How to
Take Advantage
of the People Who Are Trying to
Take Advantage
of You

50 Ways to Capitalize on the System

Joseph Stephen Breese Morse

With Eric Robert Morse

How to Take Advantage of the People Who Are Trying to Take Advantage of You.
50 Ways to Capitalize on the System. Copyright © 2006 by Joseph Stephen Breese Morse.
All Rights Reserved. Printed in the United States of America. No part of this book may
be used or reproduced in any manner whatsoever without written consent by the author.
Exceptions are granted for brief quotations within critical articles or reviews.

This book was produced by Amelior Publishing Company, an imprint of
Code Publishing, San Diego, CA.

ISBN 1-60020-040-0

978-1-60020-040-3

To Stephanie A. Morse
for teaching me the value of things.

Contents

Author's Note

It's a hectic, money-driven, dog-eat-dog world out there and it seems like everyone is trying to take advantage of everyone else. This book is about the many ways people and companies try to take advantage of us, how to avoid falling into their marketing and financial traps, and how to beat them at their own game. It's a personal finance manual as well as a history of certain institutions that have come to take advantage of us as consumers, workers, and citizens. It's a modern book because it takes into account the technological and social structures of today and is intended for a technologically advanced population, but the principles used throughout the book are based in fundamental economics, the roots of which can be seen as far back as the dawn of marketing and commerce.

To illustrate the universal nature of this book's central concept, I'd like to share a story that goes back a few hundred years. In 1722, a young print shop apprentice decided to do something radical; he became a vegetarian. His intent wasn't necessarily based on animal rights, though this apprentice was especially compassionate for his day. He did it partly because of a distaste for meat but also for economical reasons. You see, though vegetarianism wasn't the most enjoyable of diets (especially before the modern delights of Tofurky), it did cost a lot less than eating steaks every night. By the apprentice's calculations, vegetarianism cost less than half of the normal diet's price.

It was customary in the 18th century for a tradesman to pay

for his apprentices' room and board, and, noting the opportunity for savings, our young print student decided to make an offer. If the tradesman would pay him for food instead of paying the cook directly, he would take only half of what the tradesman used to pay. At such a bargain, the tradesman couldn't resist.

What the young apprentice soon realized was that with his daily food allowance, he was able to eat exactly what he wanted and he had money left over for other personal use. A fan of scholarship, the apprentice mainly bought books with his newfound extra income. And, not only did this new arrangement afford the apprentice extra money, but he was also able to capitalize on the free time he had while the tradesman and other workers walked down the street to eat their meals. While the printer was taking advantage of the savings he now had, the young apprentice was saving time *and* making money, while eating perfectly well. This young apprentice's name was Benjamin Franklin and he can rightly be considered one of the first in history to take advantage of the people who were trying to take advantage of him.

Ben Franklin eventually became synonymous with the principles this book is based on: cleverness, frugality, and industry. One would be amazed at how much these three principles do for one's wealth and, ultimately happiness, as Franklin would surely attest.

While Abraham Lincoln graces the copper coin that in turn graces the cover of this book, it almost seems more fitting that Franklin should be on the one cent piece, especially when compared to the $100 bill on which his image does appear. It was the prudent Franklin who said, "A penny saved is a penny earned." And it was he who warned that, "Necessity never made a good bargain." His heart and spirit are found throughout this book and it is my hope that I have created something worthy of his values if not his literary skill. The proof of that will be readers who can better their lives in perhaps just a few ways by capitalizing on the system.

There are a few notes that I'd like to make. First, the techniques listed in this book have been collectively named *Ad-in* techniques so as to limit the times that you must read the wordy title. The name Ad-in refers to a tennis term meaning, "my advantage," and will be explained in Part One.

Second, the figures of the amount of money saved or earned mentioned at the end of each chapter are meant as a loose guide and vary from case to case due to the many factors involved. These figures should be seen as an estimate of what you can earn yourself, but by no means are they meant as a guarantee. Also, the tally at the end of each part includes individual transactions as well as monthly and annual savings/earnings. The inconsistency is due to the nature of the techniques and the wide variety of transactions they involve. Unfortunately this is the best way to represent the myriad types of transactions; have fun calculating your own savings!

Third, the economical nature of this material begs for numerous figures and statistics, all of which require notes and citations. To save the reader (and me) from getting bogged down by footnotes, I've compiled all of the citations in the back under "Notes".

I owe a tremendous amount to Francesca Del George for editing and helping me clarify many of my ideas throughout the book and to Kristen Depken who was an immense help in editing and helping me appear to know how to speak English. I'd also like to thank my brother, Eric Robert Morse for contributing, editing, and generally raising the level of quality throughout of the book to something worth reading. I couldn't have done it without you.

I hope you enjoy reading this book as much as I have enjoyed writing it and I hope you can prosper from the techniques as much or more than I have while developing them. Now, on to *How To Take Advantage of the People Who Are Trying to Take Advantage of You*.

Part One

How to Take Advantage of the People Who Are Trying to Take Advantage of You

"A penny saved is a penny earned."

- Benjamin Franklin

"When someone asks you, a penny for your thoughts, and you put your two cents in, what happens to the other penny?"

- George Carlin

Right now, there are people trying to get your money. In fact, just about everyone is trying to get a piece of your monetary pie. This is not a scare tactic; it's just a basic characteristic of economics. You have money and, as a natural response to the market system, everyone else is trying to get it from you.

Okay, so not everyone you see throughout the day is holding out the change jar to you, but they probably work for companies who are trying to sell you products in order to get your money. These people and companies don't even care if you have money now; they'll take money from your future, and your kids' future, by way of credit and debt. From people on the street to the government to international corporations to mom and pop stores, everyone wants your money.

Unless you have spent the last 300 years on the moon, you have probably noticed this trend. Still, it is helpful to recognize it for what it is because it's easy to become complacent about money and we, as Westerners, tend to give it up freely, even when a high interest rate is attached to those purchases. This can be seen in the level of debt Americans face.

From a report released in early 2006, it has been determined that the average American household has $7,271 in revolving debt (mainly from credit cards). The entire country owes $799.1 billion, which may seem like a big, but not terrifying, number. If you don't think that number is terrifying, think of it in these terms: you could lay that many one dollar bills end to end in a line and circle the Earth 3,109 times. Based on this figure of high revolving debt, it appears that they *have* gotten your money, and then some. Sure, you may have a nice Bonde storage combination from Ikea or great memories and pictures from that family vacation to Wally World to show for it, but if you're like most Westerners, especially Americans, you don't have any savings and you have a lot of debt.

A fascinating thing about your debt is that you may not have even noticed that "they" did this to you. Many people don't, and it's no wonder because we have an abstract financial system that makes people unaware of what they spend and how they relate it to what they have earned. Unlike bartering, which consists of two parties trading two different goods that are worth more to the person who's receiving them, we trade goods for *money*, which only has *assumed* value. In fact, the actual value of a dollar bill and a ten-dollar bill is the same, which is what it costs to produce (about 3.8 cents). Nothing of substance is being lost when we buy something with a dollar, just assumed value.

Often, we don't even use physical money at all; we just trade numbers (e.g. with a debit card number) for goods. Those numbers have an infinitely smaller intrinsic value than even that of a dollar bill. I don't think we can make it more abstract than that. What results is a populace that can't accurately judge the value of the money it makes or spends.

We work for a large chunk of our day and after a couple weeks of doing that we receive a piece of paper that tells us what all that work was for. It is just a number and many people don't really associate it with the work they did; it's just a series of digits. Then, after the bank teller punches a few keys, this important number is mystically transported from your pay stub to your bank account.

From there, you may watch it as it mingles with other numbers and increases and decreases, and heaven forbid, perhaps turns red every once in a while. That is the extent to which most people think about that number. They certainly don't think about it when they see something that they want to buy. They don't think about it when they are shopping with friends, buying another round of drinks, or filling their gas tank.

When most people see something they want that their paycheck amount can't cover, another magical number suddenly appears: the sixteen digit credit card number. Why suffer in a world without the latest gadget when Uncle Chase and old Aunt Bank of America will gladly provide for us? Credit allows our eyes to write checks that our bank accounts can't cash.

Our urge to spend money we don't have is an understandable feeling. We live in a financially abstract society where it's hard to grasp where the money comes from, where it goes, and how we can take real physical things like apples and stereos just by swiping a plastic card. Based on this bizarre ritual of economics, it's almost a natural inclination to go into debt.

However easy it may be to charge away, it's not necessarily healthy, financially or otherwise. High debt can lower one's credit rating, making it more difficult to buy a home or car. It can increase the risk of bankruptcy and it usually ends up costing a fortune in interest rates just to maintain the debt. That usually results in high blood pressure, though the connection hasn't been scientifically proven. These are real consequences that will affect the way you live if they are not avoided.

Credit card companies charge hefty fees when you have enough debt, and unfortunately, they're rarely forgiving if you happen to forget a payment every once in a while. And big credit card companies aren't sympathetic to their consumers who are confused by the abstract nature of the credit trade. The excuse, "It's just a little number on a sheet of paper!" won't fly with them, unfortunately. If you are careless with your debt, you could end up giving the credit card companies a lot of little numbers on lots of sheets of paper. All of the numbers that you get on your paycheck will go to the bank companies if you're not diligent in maintaining your finances.

No matter how bad it is for us consumers, the credit card companies will still attempt to lock us in a financial stranglehold—they depend on it.

In the early 1950s, when Diners Club and American Express issued the nation's first charge cards, the owners had to pay off the balance every month. A few years later, however, Bank of America decided to allow its customers to carry a balance in what the bank termed *revolving credit*. This balance incurred interest and soon became the most profitable aspect of the credit card industry.

The card that Bank of America issued, which later became Visa, revolutionized the banking industry. Banks could now make money on a seemingly natural urge of Americans—to spend more than they have. And so credit card companies began to take advantage of us.

As can be expected, timing played a role. At the dawn of the major credit card industry in the United States, a large portion of the American populace was coming home from World War II and the Korean War. The chairman of Citibank at the time, Walter Wriston explained that we Americans, "Just put five years of our lives in a brown suit carrying an M1 rifle, and we want the refrigerator now." Credit card companies obliged and made money off of this immediate desire for houseware.

That's not fair, some may say. Credit cards shouldn't be able to make that much money on us when it's such an abstract system and it's so difficult to keep track of money. But they keep on making money on us and taking advantage of our natural urges and even our naïveté. This happens because credit card companies are targeting consumers that are younger and younger—getting to them before they fully understand the concept of debt and what it means to us later in life. College graduates commonly enter the real world now, not only with school loans to pay off, but also some stout credit card loans to pay off.

You won't be shocked to hear that credit card companies aren't the only ones trying to take advantage of us all the time. From the grocery store to your cell phone company to the government, they want your money and they will take advantage of you to get to it.

They get the better of us monetarily by tuning into our needs and desires. Companies, through advertising, for example, tune into our physiological needs by showing us a warm hearty pizza around dinnertime when most people are likely to be hungry. Companies target and seek to satisfy our innate human urges in a number of ways. Another way in which companies take advantage of us is by appealing to our deep-seated social needs.

In the 1930s, Listerine made it a social crime to have *halitosis*, or bad breath, something that their product could conveniently get rid of. What most people don't realize is that halitosis is a term invented by a marketer to make the condition sound scientific and thus make Listerine seem like a more effective product.

Lifebuoy soap also tuned into people's social desires by introducing the "Beeee . . . Ohhhh," commercials. This ad campaign, which showcased the smelly people with body odor and prompted the "B.O." reference, spurred countless copycat ads from the companies in the deodorant industry including the Sure commercials, which show self-conscious commuters afraid to raise their arms because they weren't *sure* about their bodily stench. In other Sure commercials, we see all types of people (even the Statue of Liberty) raising their arms in confidence because they've defeated the social ill of the stinky underarm. When these commercials started making people think that their coworkers may be making fun of them because of their body odor, they bought more products that could prevent the dreaded B.O., especially Lifebuoy and Sure. Listerine, Lifebuoy, and Sure campaigns were very successful because they took advantage of Americans' social desires, more specifically our desires to not be known as the smelly guy in the corner cubicle at the office.

There are countless other human desires that companies try to target, of course, and they are manifold and diverse. And, for as many desires and needs that we have, there are as many or more companies that are looking to capitalize on them. Nike takes advantage of our desire to compete; Smirnoff Ice takes advantage of our desire to be popular; Victoria's Secret takes advantage of half of the population's desire to be sexy; and Apple's iPod takes advantage of our collective desire to have the coolest gadget that everyone else has.

We want the latest, greatest thing, and we don't want to wait until we've saved enough money for it. We also want to make our lives easier and give ourselves more time for all the new stuff we've just bought with our credit cards. We want all of that, but of course we still want the great deal, the bargain.

We want to say that we got our great shoes at a dramatic discount. We want to say that the Kelley Blue Book value of that car was $500 over what we paid. We want to say that we got the first month in our new apartment for free. We want to have the satisfaction of knowing someone at the grocery store down the street paid 50 cents more for his grapes.

We want the bargain, and surprisingly, of all the things that companies will take advantage of you for, your desire for the deal is the easiest. If the company or organization can convince you that you are getting a bargain, you will be eager to pay them for it.

A play I recently saw, "Three Little Angels," demonstrates this beautifully. A business-savvy character is compelled to briefly run the store of a naïve business owner. The owner is dumbfounded when the guest sells an item that hadn't even been looked at in years.

"How did you get that much?" the owner asked the salesman.

"I marked on it with an ink pen," the salesman explained.

"What? I don't understand," the owner said.

"The customer wasn't going to spend the regular price of $20 for the suit, but he was eager to pay the *marked-down* price of $20 for a suit with a small blemish!"

You may think that this doesn't happen in the real world though. Just because someone in a theatrical play can manipulate a buyer's spending habits, you may think that it's not likely to happen at your favorite store. You may be surprised to find out that it happens all the time.

When stores want to sell more of an item, they routinely mark the price down and slap a "SALE" sign on the item. Sometimes, however, when they do this, they forget to actually mark the price down and the item on sale costs the same as it did when it wasn't on sale. The amazing thing is that researchers have found that the artificial sale price compels just as many people to buy the product as the real sale price.

It turns out that people are just interested in the word "sale", not in the actual price.

A study conducted by the University of Illinois—Chicago Center for Urban Economic Development found that 6.4% of all the items paid for in Chicago-area Wal-Mart stores were incorrectly priced. But rarely do you see the complaints. How many times do you audit *your* grocery bill? It occurred to me once at the grocery store to do so, and I immediately found an incorrectly priced cereal box. At $1.33 a box more than the marked sale price, that really added up, considering I bought thirty boxes. Most people don't audit their checkout process though. That's why another study by the University of California—Berkeley found that 8.3% of items in all stores across California were priced incorrectly. If we're content with paying the wrong price (often more than advertised), stores like Wal-Mart, Target, and Costco aren't going to do much to fix the problem. We want the deal so badly, we don't even check to make sure it's legitimate and we're actually getting it.

The idea of a bargain is very compelling, even when it doesn't really exist. In the case of the stores mentioned above, the wrong prices are probably accidental, but most companies actually use the ploy of the bargain or, better yet, an artificial bargain to make sales. They use the bait of a bargain to lure us consumers in so that they can make money on us. Most retail stores have perfected this tactic to a science and use it constantly. Every time I go into a Macy's, for instance, it seems that there is a sale. Either I'm a really lucky shopper or the department store is always using the ploy of a sale to get us to buy their merchandise.

Sometimes, when companies or people make an offer to lure you in, it's a true bargain. That is, the product really is worth more than the offer price. The good buy, however, would be for a limited time only, and if you continued buying the product or service, you'd end up paying the regular price or more after the initial trial is over. It could be that the company uses the bargain to draw you into larger purchases. Either way, they intend to get your money; otherwise they wouldn't be offering you the deal.

The grocery store by my office, for instance, regularly has great deals. They usually have seasonal fruit for unheard of prices. When most people see the signs in front of the store proclaiming "Navel Oranges 20¢ a Pound!" they are compelled to enter. Once they're in the store, of course, they end up spending much more than 20¢ a pound for oranges. They buy drinks, meat, bread products, and more at regular prices or higher. Even if the store loses money with the oranges, they end up making a lot more money with the other items that people buy.

It seems obvious that to fully take advantage of the bargain, one should limit his purchase to what's on sale and to what he needs. But it's hard to deny yourself other items especially if they're things you need, and besides, it probably wouldn't be worthwhile to go to a store for just one item. And so companies like my local grocery store can continue to rely on those additional purchases.

Similar techniques are used in bulk grocery stores like Costco. Some of you may be familiar with seizing bargains that were too good to be true, however you may not have wanted to walk out with a two-gallon container of mayonnaise, enough to feed a small army. Bulk discounts are examples of how companies lure customers in with a deal and usually make more than they would at the regular size. It is also an example of how consumers must be wary of deals. If you don't have a small army, you might have to throw away over half of the tub of condiment and it may end up costing more than it would have if you had purchased the smaller jar, which is more expensive per ounce.

By purchasing just the oranges at 20¢ a pound, as in the case above, and by buying the smaller can of mayonnaise instead of the waste-inducing vat from Costco, you are doing two things. First, you are acknowledging the ploys that the companies are using to take advantage of you, and second, you are taking advantage of them. This is one basic example of the principles described in this book. What will result from your diligence in taking advantage of those who are trying to take advantage of you is a wealthier lifestyle full of more money and a lot more perks.

But paying attention to deals at grocery stores isn't going to make you rich, and that's not what I'm trying to show. Though I will mention grocery habits again briefly, this book is not about how to find the best deals at the grocery store. It is about helping you take control of your economic situation in many aspects of the financial world through the countless techniques I will explain, and part of that means understanding what the grocery store deals (to name one) are attempting to do. There are myriad ways that people and companies are trying to lure you in and take advantage of you, some obvious and some psychologically cunning, but with these pages, you will have the power to turn the tables on those commercial entities and learn how to take advantage of them.

If that sounds unethical to you, it's not. You won't be stealing anything, though it may feel that way when your credit card starts paying you for instance. You won't be doing anything that the average Joe wouldn't do if he knew how to do it. Most readers will not feel bad about getting multi-billion dollar companies to give back a little, but if you're hesitant, don't be. Those companies are giving you these deals and bargains because they want to take advantage of *you*, so why should you feel bad about taking advantage of them? You shouldn't.

There is a valid concern that if enough people start to do any of the techniques that I describe in this book, the companies involved will stop giving you the opportunities. That is a possibility, but until that happens, you might as well be taking advantage of them while you can. Additionally, it's possible that the types of marketing techniques that companies are using to get your business will always be there because there will always be another company offering the same deal in order to gain market share.

It may seem like this book recommends that you nickel and dime your way to financial success, but that's certainly not the point. It recommends that you *penny* your way to financial success. Just kidding. True, some of the techniques that I suggest in this book are small and won't make you rich, but as a great founding father has been credited with saying, "A penny saved is a penny earned." There is great value in small things, such as a penny, when applied wisely, and that founding father should know.

It's true that another great American graces the U.S. one-cent piece, but Benjamin Franklin would be a much more appropriate figure on such a monetary unit. It is he who embodies the value of the penny. After all, it was Franklin who said, "If you would be wealthy, think of saving as well as getting." And, concerning wealth, "When the well's dry, we know the worth of water." But he also knew that money wasn't everything and that it was a means to the end of other great things. He said to be rich, you must be content and he also noted in a poke at the greedy, "He that is of the opinion money will do everything may well be suspected of doing everything for money."

Great Franklin quotes are easy to come by and are scattered throughout this book, and they all point to a few central themes: frugality, industry, and thoughtfulness. Frugality, though, was Franklin's chief virtue. It was prominent in his quest for moral perfection, seen in his words, "Frugality: Make no expense but to do good to others or yourself (i.e. waste nothing)." It is for this virtue that Franklin's appearance on the $100 bill is ironic. While he did become a wealthy man later in life, he was anything but showy or ostentatious. His wife had to surprise him with a china bowl and silver spoon one morning at breakfast because he wouldn't have had them otherwise. Franklin's wife, Deborah, had the, "excuse," that, "her husband deserved a silver spoon and china bowl as well as any of his neighbors."

Indeed, through his fiscal virtues and diligence, Benjamin Franklin did become a very wealthy man. His maxims reflect his journey from poverty to wealth and have been cited by nearly everyone, and his likeness graces the logos of numerous financial institutions. Using his enlightened viewpoint, I'd like to describe a fascinating thought experiment involving the penny.

The penny has had it pretty rough lately. You'll often see the one-cent pieces littering sidewalks and sofas and no one has the industry to pick them up. It's just not worth it to collect such an insignificant amount of money, one may say, referring to the diminutive monetary unit.

The homeless people that brighten our walks through downtown reject pennies (I've actually experienced a homeless person rejecting anything smaller than a $20 bill). The Federal government is considering abolishing pennies altogether and some countries, like Australia, already go without the one-cent piece, rounding everything up or down to the nearest five cents. The value of a penny has been under serious scrutiny recently.

And it's hard to imagine how many times you'd have to pick up a penny to make a serious impact on your financial situation. If a person were to save a penny a day for an entire year, he would have just $3.65 at the end of the year. That couldn't even buy you a grande mocha ay-caramba latte at your favorite coffee shop. A penny's nothing. Or is it?

If you think a penny is worthless, it may shock you to learn that if someone saved just one penny each day for his entire life and gained interest in an average-yield fund (compounded just once annually), he would end up with $19,653.14 by the time he retired. A penny a day may not seem like anything to blow your nose at, but twenty grand may catch your attention.

This hypothetical demonstrates the crux of this book. Franklin said, "Little strokes fell great oaks." And that applies to personal finance as much as it does to forestry. A little ingenuity and guile financially can go a long way. By learning how to take advantage of the people who are taking advantage of you, you should be able to learn the true value of things and, in turn, live a very comfortable lifestyle.

It is important to be clear that I am not a financial wizard or even a financial expert, though I do understand the major trends within the economy and practice meticulous personal finance. The reader should be aware that Fidelity Investments or any other financial institution has not endorsed the techniques found in this book. I am a middle-class consumer, just like many of the readers and most of the Western world, and being so, I guarantee that the ideas expressed in this book work for us.

I am not claiming that this book will make you rich or make you the king of a small country by any means, though I am researching the latter. What the ideas in this book offer, however, are a considerable amount of financial freedom, endless amounts of perks, and the peace of mind in knowing that you're not falling for some great trick being played out there. You don't have to be the corporations' marionette anymore.

You can have several Fortune 500 companies and even the government bending over backward to accommodate you. Sounds nice for a change, doesn't it? That is the point of this book.

The main principle of *Taking Advantage of the People Who Are Trying to Take Advantage of You* is simple. Companies use psychological tools and offer bargains to the public, through which they may come out even or perhaps lose money. Then, they make a switch and begin making money on you, usually a lot more than they lost. Your job is to take them up on their offer or marketing ploy, make the most of it, then discontinue the deal before the switch, all of which is legal, honest, and profitable. It is your money you're dealing with after all, not the corporations'. The companies want something you have, so it only makes sense that you should make them work for it.

This book will describe the major financial institutions you are most likely working with and describe the techniques that will help you make the most of those business relationships. We'll review credit card companies and other banks, home and car purchases, retail and grocery stores, the Internet, government and taxes, and the workplace, all of which contribute to your being taken advantage of in different ways. This book will help you acknowledge that and beat them at their own game. Once you learn how to take advantage of the people who are trying to take advantage of you, you'll be on your way to the world of a million perks and financial control. You'll be able to earn profits off of those credit card companies, fly round-trip across the country for $39, and maximize your tax return. You'll be able to make $180 an hour (if only briefly), get a state-of-the-art cellular telephone for free, and make the bank pay *you*. In all, the earnings and savings from the techniques in this book come to just over $100,000. That should be enough to make you want to learn more.

The main principle of this book may sound fairly straightforward, but it will require some important skills that may not be the easiest to come by. They include patience, conscientiousness, communication, organization, and to round it off, it helps to have technological skills and some math skills. Don't be alarmed by all these requirements. I will present tips to help you achieve these skills as you learn about the rewarding concepts out there.

I will go on to reveal some very interesting bargains and offers that some companies are giving us and explain techniques that will show you how to fully take advantage of those offers. But before I get started, I want to make this book a little easier to read. I realize that the title is a bit lengthy and would be obtrusive if I kept using it to represent the main idea. Instead of repeating the concept of taking advantage of people who are trying to take advantage of you, I've come up with a concise term for the broad idea. It comes from the sport of tennis, where I've dug deep into the terminology for an appropriate term. When the tennis player who's serving is winning at one point in the game, he has the *advantage*. When this happens, the winning player can claim, "Ad–in." Throughout the book, I'll refer to the concept of *taking advantage of the people who are trying to take advantage of you* as Ad–in.

To fully capitalize on the techniques of Ad–in (see how easy that flows?), it helps to be able to take a little risk. Of course, there are variations of all of the techniques reflecting different risk standards, but to fully enjoy the benefits of the principles in this book you will need to take a little risk. Does that mean that I want you to gamble your house on a pyramid scheme? Of course not! You will come to see that the techniques that I suggest in this book are time-tested and guaranteed to help you financially.

Of course there is risk in the techniques that I am describing, but there's risk in everything everyone does. My ideas are no different in that respect, but few people do them, which may make them seem more risky. They're not. Just because every one of your neighbors fails to follow these guidelines doesn't mean that they're too risky. In fact, Ad–in works *because* none of your neighbors practice it. The organizations and companies rely on people giving them their money, and if everyone took advantage of them, they would stop offering people great deals.

It goes without saying that with skills like patience, conscientiousness, communication, and organization, you will be able to minimize your risk. Even if you don't want to incur risk, the concepts in this book will still benefit you and allow you to maintain sounder finances.

Now, let's get into the techniques of *Taking Advantage of the People Who Are Trying to Take Advantage of You,* and you'll have hundreds of companies at your beck and call before you can say the title of this book.

Franklin Says:
"Keep thy shop and thy shop will keep you"

At the end of each chapter, there will be a brief summary of the preceding chapter. I'll break down what financial institution or institutions we spoke of in the chapter and the traits or behaviors that they target in taking advantage of us. I'll also describe what skills are useful in taking advantage of those institutions and the overall monetary benefit you'll receive by using the Ad-In techniques (shown in *What Ben Earned*). Enjoy!

Part Two

The Debt Benefit

"Some debts are fun when you are acquiring them, but none are fun when you set about retiring them"

- Ogden Nash

If I owe you a pound, I have a problem; but if I owe you a million, the problem is yours."

- John Maynard Keynes

I'm a deadbeat.

No, that doesn't mean that I'm a good-for-nothing loafer who sleeps on my friend's couch and plays video games in my bathrobe with the shades closed all day while my friend works. Nor does it mean that I have left my theoretical children in the lurch while an ex-wife struggles to get by. None of that applies to me, but to some, I'm considered a deadbeat. That's what some people in the credit card industry call those of us who pay their card balance in full every month and don't involuntarily donate their hard-earned money to the creditors in the form of interest and finance charges. This should illustrate the fond feelings that most people in the credit card industry have for their customers.

Of course, they do have a fondness for the revolvers—those

who constantly have a balance and thus tend to pay interest on it. Revolvers are what industry insiders call the sweet spot in the pool of consumers. Banks make most of their profits on this type of consumer, a population that seems to be growing in popularity. As mentioned in the introduction, the average debt that consumers in this country maintain is increasing like the average waistline. And not so surprising, as our collective debt goes up, so does the number of complaints issued to the Better Business Bureau about individual credit card companies every year. The Better Business Bureau (BBB) is a not-for-profit organization that works as a consumer advocate group to report on millions of businesses and charities, and it's one of our options as consumers to complain about inappropriate billing or fraudulent behavior. Credit cards were the subject of a record number of complaints to the BBB last year, slightly beating out Cheesy Used-Car Dealers and Phony Baloney Pyramid Schemes.

At the time of this writing, the BBB reported 1,566 complaints for Bank of America alone that were resolved over the past 12 months, mostly concerning billing. Other banks were similarly reported. Citigroup had 669 complaints reported in the last year and Chase Manhattan received 1,780 complaints for the same time period. By contrast, General Motors, the third largest corporation in the US, received 50 complaints in the last year and just 88 in the past 36 months.

Even if you weren't one of the thousands of consumer advocates who issued one of those complaints to the BBB, it's still likely that you've had difficult times with your credit card as well, especially if you find yourself in the category the creditors have named revolvers. But while our frustration with these companies continues to grow, so does our business with them. Why do we find it so easy, yet so hard to do business with companies like these—ones that take so much of our money without so much as a thank you card to show for it? It may help to take a look at the history of the industry and how it has been able to take advantage of us in such a significant way.

We already touched on the history of credit cards in the introduction, but I'd like to support that with a brief story about the industry, which is one of the largest in both the United States and the world for that matter. The major credit card companies made $30 billion in 2005 alone, and most of that was on the interest of the revolving debt that we've racked up. The banks that lend us money have pushed the envelope on what the American consumer is willing to spend and how much debt they're willing to incur. Who could have predicted twenty years ago that a large portion of the population now can't live without their 700-inch plasma TV or their dog that can fit in a purse? And that consumerism would turn out to be bad news for our personal finances.

On the positive side, the flexibility offered with such debt helps to fuel the economy, especially in times of economic recession. During the dot-com bust and subsequent economic downturn, consumer spending kept up its pace and basically supported the economy, along with the housing industry, making it a relatively short recession. One could argue that credit card companies like Chase, Citicard, Bank of America, and others have helped the economy by allowing us consumers to spend like we just cashed in on a lot of Exxon Mobile stock.

So the industry, it seems, is a double-edged sword. Like I mentioned in the introduction, credit card companies have taken advantage of the consumer's urge to consume and his ability to ignore debt and, as a result, Americans are piling up balances, content in just paying their low monthly payments (a habit that makes most financial advisors contemplate giving up their profession and joining Cirque de Soleil).

To demonstrate, I'd like to describe a common situation in the modern age of paying down the seemingly ubiquitous debt that most Americans have. Let's say Bob, a hypothetical credit card spender, just bought an obscene amount of beef jerky and now has the same amount of revolving debt as the average American, $7,271, and pays the minimum payment each month (2% of the total). In this hypothetical, it would take Bob over five years to pay off his card if he never added any debt to it—and that's if his credit card has a fairly decent APR of 6.9%. An APR, or Annual Percentage Rate, is the rate at which the credit loan accrues interest, usually falling into the range of 5%-25%. Most APRs are much higher than Bob's rate mentioned above— they're generally around 19%. With a higher rate like that, it would take almost *eight* years for Bob to pay for all of his beef jerky. All the while, Bob would be making some already wealthy people even wealthier through interest. Bob is supporting a giant industry that is growing larger by the second.

The fascinating thing is that the enormous industry of credit was nearly crushed out of existence in the late '70s and early '80s. During that time, inflation was extremely high and prices were increasing over 13% from year to year by 1979. Interest rates were also very high—banks were charging other banks 20% to borrow money. To put that in perspective, inflation for 2005 was about 3% and banks nowadays charge around 4% to loan money. Suffice it to say that the rates in the '70s were very high comparatively.

One would think, for the credit card industry, those high rates would be good, and they were good to an extent. Theoretically, the higher the interest rates, the more money those companies could charge their customers and the more profit they could make. The rates that those companies charged their customers generally kept pace with the rising interest rates they were paying other banks. But there were laws in most states that prohibited companies from charging their customers exorbitantly high interest rates. These usury laws, as they are called, prohibited New York companies, like Citibank, from charging more than 12% on their credit card loans. However, the Citibank still had to pay the Federal Reserve Bank or other banks 20% for the money they owed because the usury laws didn't apply to businesses, thus credit companies found themselves in a crunch — sometimes losing 8% on this unequal system.

The credit companies were going broke as a result. Walter Wriston of Citibank put it this way, "You are lending money at 12 percent and paying 20 percent, you don't have to be Einstein to realize you're out of business."

Credit card companies started charging annual fees, but that wasn't enough to cover their enormous losses. By 1980, Citibank had lost over $1 billion. That's not chump change, even for behemoths like Citibank. Those companies had to look elsewhere for ideas and a solution came in the least likely of places with respect to world economics: South Dakota.

In 1980, South Dakota passed legislation that allowed banks within its borders to charge its customers an unlimited APR on their debt. That legislation, coupled with a Supreme Court case that allowed banks to charge people in other states what they could charge in their home state, led the way for a booming credit card industry.

South Dakota's governor at the time recalled in an interview that people were giving a lot of credit (no pun intended) to his state for reviving the industry. "That South Dakota saved Citibank: I believe it did," Wriston said.

There are a few other states like South Dakota that have no cap on the interest they can charge. If you look on your credit card statement or bill, you will notice the address is in one of these states. Delaware, which has no cap, is the home to MBNA, JP Morgan Chase, Morgan Stanley (which operates Discover), and HSBC. Providian is located in New Hampshire, Capital One is based in Virginia, and American Express is located in Utah. All of these states allow the banks to charge whatever they please for their loans. Theoretically, the interest rates for cards with these companies could be 100% or higher (yes, it's possible). However, I don't see that happening. Even in the free-market economies of the world, or perhaps especially in the free-market economies, people have a tendency to punish greed, even when they could stand to profit a little from someone else's greed.

In economics, there is an experimental game, which proves this concept time and time again: it's called the ultimatum game. In the game, two parties interact anonymously and only once for a monetary transaction. They only interact once so that reciprocation won't be an issue. One of the two people gets to decide how to split a sum of money, let's say $10, between the two players in any proportion. The money is a reward for playing the game and does not originate from either of the players. After the first person offers how to split the money, player two decides whether or not to accept the offer. If player two accepts the offer by player one, both players keep the amounts designated by player one. On the other hand, if player two rejects the offer, neither player gets any of the cash.

Imagine if you were playing this game and it was up to you to decide the amount of money to split between yourself and the other player. If you're like most people, you would offer an equitable split of five dollars each. However, when this game is conducted in labs, participants sometimes offer less than $5 to their compatriot. When the offers from the first player get down to about $2 for player two ($8 for player one), they are usually rejected. This is bizarre because, theoretically, it would be wise for the second player to accept anything the first player offers because anything would be more than what he had before and more than what he would receive if he rejects the offer. It's almost as if the second player in this game wants to teach player one a lesson when he or she offers an inequitable amount.

It may be a different story if the values are higher. Teaching someone a lesson is a lot easier for most people if it costs them $1 as opposed to $100. However, according to studies, this lesson actually makes the teacher feel good. The act of punishing one's counterpart in such a game stimulates the part of the brain associated with the dopamine pathway. In essence, punishing someone for being greedy makes us feel good. Regardless of how it makes us feel, we nonetheless reject greed, even when we could stand to profit a small bit from it. Hence, most people would avoid using credit cards with 100% interest rates, even if it helped us to get the new iPod now. It actually makes us feel good to reject companies that charge so much—even more than the iPod does.

So, we probably won't see rates above 50% in the near future, but we are stuck with some fairly high rates anyway. You can thank the states without usury laws for the 20-30% rates we do see now. You can also, perhaps, thank the Delawares and South Dakotas for keeping those credit cards afloat through historically high-interest periods.

But can you blame South Dakota for your massive credit card debt? Not so fast. South Dakota and Citibank were just looking out for their best interests (again, no pun intended). South Dakota needed jobs and Citibank wanted to stay in business and make money. Do you blame them? They were taking advantage of their customers' Americanism, but they were doing what most Americans are trying to do themselves—just make a living. Until now, you can only blame yourself for your high credit card debt on high interest cards. You were being taken advantage of and not taking advantage of those companies. Returning to our tennis jargon, this would be called Ad-Out.

An interesting aspect about the industry is that the APRs of major credit cards increased as inflation and the Federal Fund Rate went up, however, they didn't *decrease* when those other rates went down in the eighties. Customers didn't seem to mind or notice the imbalance and just went right on paying the astronomical rates along with their annual fees. The credit card companies were making a killing.

Recently, as mentioned above, the Federal Fund Rate has

been historically low. The Federal Fund Rate is the rate at which the Federal Reserve (or the Fed) lends money to banks. That rate has a waterfall effect on every other rate in the country including mortgage rates, car loans, savings account interest rates, and APRs for credit card companies. If the Federal Reserve Rate goes down, other APRs will inevitably go down as well.

Since the Federal Fund Rate is so low now, credit card companies can give us great deals to attract us as customers. And those deals are at the heart of the first technique I will describe.

1. How low can they go?

You may have begun to ignore the endless offers that you receive in the mail for new credit cards. For some, you are pre-approved; for others, you have a whopping $20,000 potential credit limit. Many credit card companies have now taken AT&T's lead and begun offering cards with no annual fees (AT&T offered the first card without an annual fee in the '90s). Other mailers offer you a card with a small annual fee, but give you great rewards like miles on your favorite airline. A recent trend in credit offers is a low introductory rate on balance transfers.

If you resist the urge to dump your usual bundle of junk mail in the trash, you may be able to save yourself a lot of money. Credit card companies, in 2004, spent over $1 billion on advertising and over $4 billion in direct marketing to get your attention.

Jacqueline Morse, a dear relative of mine, has been getting junk mail for a few years now, from coupon mailers to political advertisements. She's even gotten magazine subscriptions that she didn't really ask for. Of course, she gets credit card promotions too. Recently, she just got an offer to open up an American Express card with no annual fee, a $25 start-up gift, and a low 3.8% APR.

Jacqueline would have been ecstatic, except Jacqueline doesn't exist. I invented her to determine where certain junk mail promotions get my address. It's pretty clear now that when you give your address to a company, you can be sure that they will offer that address to other companies, sometimes credit card companies. Pretty soon they will all be sending you offers.

Among other things, the high volume of credit card offers in the mail is an indication that there is an enormous amount of competition in the industry. And competition usually leads to great bargains for the target market. Of course, the amount of money that these companies spend on marketing pales in comparison to the amount of money they earn, so it makes a lot of sense to them. You can take advantage of this heated competition.

Let's look at the hypothetical Sally for an example of a credit card revolver. Sally has one credit card with a $10,000 balance on it. She pays a good chunk of money to the credit card company every month ($200) but that's just the minimum she must pay. She has a high APR on that card and is incurring a finance charge of $170 every month, so she's only really paying off $30 a month. At this rate of payment, Sally will be paying for this debt for 108 months, or 9 years! That is quite a large stretch of time.

Because Sally does not really think about it that way, she doesn't do anything about it. She looks at it as just another payment that she has to make every month to sustain her standard of living—she doesn't even remember the last time she didn't have credit card debt to pay down. She gets offers in the mail all the time asking her to sign up for a new credit card at a low APR, but she just tosses them into the trash, opting to watch E!, Entertainment Television instead.

She's not alone in disregarding these offers. Out of the 5 billion direct mail pieces that credit cards send out each year, only one-third of 1% score a reply. Sally, like most people, thinks that either the cards won't actually accept her or that getting a new card will hurt her credit rating. Or it could be that she just doesn't have time for the hassle of applying for a new card and waiting around for the response. Ironic though it is, Sally has plenty of time to work for the money that she spends every month on interest for her debt.

She's probably misinformed about all her reasons to reject the new credit card offers. If she receives an invitation to apply for a credit card, pre-qualified or not, she will usually be accepted. The banks that send out the offers intentionally send them to people who would be suitable for the card. The chances are that if you get an offer in the mail or elsewhere, you'll be accepted by the creditor.

On the other hand, Sally may think that she has too many other credit cards or that she doesn't make enough money for another credit card. But most likely, the credit card company will accept her because they are trying to make money and the easiest method to do that is to get more customers. If anything, she might receive a lower than expected credit line, but most likely, she'll get the new card.

Having one more card doesn't dramatically hurt her credit rating either — it actually may help. When a bank looks at your credit report, they like to see consistent payment on time, but if the customer has had no opportunities to pay on time (i.e. if they have few or no credit cards), his or her rating may be lower. More cards equal more opportunity for good credit. The number of credit inquiries and number of accounts open do affect one's credit rating, but all of that new credit information accounts for only 10% of your credit score. A much larger percentage (30%) is based on the amount owed, and that amount is in proportion to the total credit line.

This is an important factor to keep in mind: the amount of debt a person has compared with his or her credit limit, the debt to credit ratio. A high ratio is bad for your credit score and maxing out is very detrimental. If Sally had a credit limit of $11,000 and her debt was at $10,000, her ratio would be at 91% and banks would see that as a red flag. Getting another card would help alleviate the problem. If Sally signed up for another card with a $4,000 limit, her debt to debt to limit ratio would be $10,000 to $15,000, or 66% as opposed to 91%.

These reasons might be nice, but let's say Sally is still skeptical about getting that new card. And anyway, she thinks, it takes so much time to fill out the forms, send in the application, and get started on a new card. But the time she spends to fill out the application, which could be as short as 10 minutes, could be well worth it because a new credit card could mean a much lower interest rate and that means that she will be saving a significant amount of money.

With her current card at 19.99% APR (which is high, but not the highest), Sally would end up paying a total of $21,660.33 on her initial balance of $10,000! That's over 200% of the initial debt. She would end up paying $11,660.33 in interest alone. Most consumers, when looking at it this way, would agree that that is unacceptable and that's probably why most credit cards don't show you the total you will end up paying. They only show you how much your monthly payments or small APR would be. If Sally were to transfer that debt to a lower APR credit card, she could be on her way to paying that debt down in no time. Her debt to credit line ratio would decrease faster and her credit score would potentially go up.

Let's say that Sally got an offer for a better APR in the mail, 9.99%, which isn't terrific, but it is better than her astronomical 19.99% card. If she transferred her balance and paid the same amount each month as she did before ($200), she could pay off the card completely in less than five and a half years, saving over three and a half years of payments. Best of all she would decrease the overall interest payment to a manageable $2,985.46. This is a striking figure. Though the new APR was just half of the first one, her savings were more than 75% of her original interest expenditure!

The bottom line is that if you have debt on a high-interest card, you are throwing money away. Even if the lower-interest offer is for a short introductory period only, you will still benefit if you apply for the new card and transfer the balance. Just make sure the APR doesn't revert to a higher rate after the introductory period ends, and you'll be saving money.

Some may think that their loyalty will pay off in the long run if they stick with their original credit cards. Some will just laugh at that statement. Unfortunately, your loyalty will only get you to pay more money, and perhaps a higher credit limit if anything. Most credit card companies will jack up the interest rate for the slightest consumer mishap, like being one day late on a payment, and the customer's years of business won't matter to the computer that automatically assigns the bright and shiny new 29.99% rate.

Many credit card companies will now increase the interest on a loan if they find that a customer has been late on some other loan, credit card, or even utility bill. The moral of the story is that credit card companies don't feel any loyalty toward their customers, so we customers should feel no loyalty toward them.

One thing to keep in mind is the fee associated with balance transfers. Usually, it's a minimum of $50 and 3% of the total amount transferred, but if you are saving $8,000 in the long run, as in Sally's case above, it is probably worth it.

It's possible that your new card would even wave the fee if it meant getting you as a new customer (this happed when I applied for a credit card for my business). If you apply for a new card on the phone, the friendly operator in India named Jimbo will ask you for the transfer amount and card from which you want to transfer a balance. At that point, ask them to wave the balance transfer fee; they may feel obliged to do so. Tell them that you can't afford to increase the debt—that's why you're transferring to a new card with a lower rate. Since they won't make any money on you unless you transfer the balance, chances are that the customer service representative may wave the fee for you. If that doesn't work, say you'll have to stay with your current card. They may change their mind, but if they don't, you can always call back and transfer the balance later with another operator.

If you do get to transfer without a balance transfer fee, audit your account and make sure they don't charge you after the transfer goes through. You should be checking your bills anyway to make sure there aren't any suspicious purchases on it, but you should certainly make sure any unexpected fees from the credit card company are absent from your statement too.

Also make sure that the rate you're transferring to is a fixed rate. The variable rate may look good at the time, but rates fluctuate in a wide range and can lead to heavy costs, especially now with the general trend in interest moving up. To find out if the offer includes a fixed or variable rate, just ask the customer service rep, or look on the back of the offer they mail you. The APR should be in large print at the top of the disclosures. It will say 16.99% variable, 9.99% fixed, or something similar. When cards say prime plus a percentage, like prime + 4.99%, it's variable.

Some financial advisors will tell you that card jumping is bad. Well, I say that financial advisors' exorbitant fees are bad. Credit card companies frown on customers who may not stay with them, but from my experience, if you have a decent credit score, companies will want your business. You'll be essentially giving a credit card a couple thousand dollars in interest (as in the case above) for nothing if you stick with high interest rates. By switching to lower interest rates, you'll be taking advantage of credit card companies by paying less.

2. Ask for a lower APR

Even if you don't get offers in the mail for low-interest credit cards, or if you are declined a new card for some reason, you can still benefit from your current credit card companies. Find the number to customer service for the company (it's usually on the back of the card), and call them up. Ask the rep if he can lower your interest rate—you may be surprised by his response.

If you're a good customer and you usually pay on time, the companies will most likely want to make you happy by lowering your interest rate. It may be just a few percentage points, but like we saw in our example with Sally, a few percentage points can go a long way in saving money.

A study conducted in 2002 showed that one 5-minute phone call to a credit card company resulted in a lower APR for 56% of customers. Those successful callers ended up receiving more than a third off of their previous APRs, from an average of 16% to an average of 10.47%.

If you haven't made a purchase in a while and you've been paying down your credit card, the company may be even more eager to lower your rate and get you purchasing again. The longer you are a customer, the more likely the chance they will lower your APR. But they won't decrease the rate on their own. You have to ask in order to receive.

I'm constantly amazed every time I ask a customer service rep what kind of offers I can receive. The offers that are proposed for the same card usually differ vastly from time to time and even from rep to rep. I asked for a better rate from one particular card and I was accidentally disconnected after I heard what their best offer was going to be. Moments later, when I called back, that same, "best offer," was reduced a whole percentage point. Why Buffy in Indonesia can offer a 0.99% APR for the life of a balance transfer and Jimbo in Botswana can only offer a 1.99% APR is beyond me. It just goes to show that you shouldn't rely on what the operator offers you as written in stone. Who knows, if I had called back and spoken with Chaz in Peru, I might have gotten an even better offer.

No matter what the nationality of the person you're speaking to, it is important that you have effective communication skills. Being able to communicate what you have and what you want is vital to Ad-in as in most business transactions.

3. Increase the credit limit on low-interest cards

If you have multiple cards, you can really start to take advantage of the people who are trying to take advantage of you. If you have been a customer of a card for a period of over a year, you should call to see if the company will increase your credit limit.

Increasing your limit does a number of positive things. First, it decreases your debt to credit ratio, which benefits your credit rating. Second, it allows you more leverage with other credit cards. If you increase the limit of a card with a lower interest rate than another card you hold, you can allow for a balance transfer that could end up saving you thousands of dollars.

Be aware of the different interest rates applied to different loans, however. One card of yours may have five different interest rates—two for purchases, one for balance transfers, one for a special offer, and one, perhaps, for the heck of it. When you increase your credit limit, ask which rate will be applied to new purchases.

Credit companies want to increase your credit limit because they think you'll want to max out your card. But, if you increase your limit and don't max out your card, you can improve your credit rating; and if you transfer the balance you can save money. It's a win/win situation.

4. Cancel cards that won't decrease your APR

If you have cards that won't lower your interest rate, you may want to cancel the card. When you tell a customer service rep that you're going to cancel, he or she will go into this robotic plea written by someone in the sixties to encourage you to stay. "Do you know that we value you as a customer and want to ensure that you're happy…" After all the sappy, "we're sorry to see you go," mumbo jumbo, they may reconsider lowering your interest rate after all. I've done this a number of times, all with the same result. When you ask for the lower rate and the customer service rep refuses, explain that you'll have to cancel. The rep may give you another offer to try to retain your business, like a free magazine subscription, free debt protector service for a month, or a nifty clock radio worth $5. If those offers don't entice you (they shouldn't), tell the rep that you still want to cancel.

The rep will then direct you to a resolution specialist who will go in to all the real offers that may entice you — 3.99% for a limited time, or 5.99% for the life of the loan. Now we're talkin'! It costs credit card companies, on average, around $100 to gain a customer. If they spent that much on you and are at the risk of losing your business, they will try almost everything to get you to stay.

If you decline their offers at this point, they will most likely accept the cancellation of the card. Unfortunately, there isn't another supervisor after the resolution specialist who will offer you a better APR or a free car or anything.

To increase your leverage when speaking to the resolution specialist, you may want to pay off your credit card either by transferring the amount to another card or paying down the balance. If you have nowhere to go with your debt, you can still cancel the card, but you will need to continue paying them every month. Also, if you cancel your card while you still have a balance, the company may increase the interest rate as a penalty. Like piranhas feeding on vulnerable prey, the company that has given you credit will sense blood in the water if you cancel your card while you still have a balance. The company assumes that you are in trouble financially and it isn't usually willing to help you out of trouble.

Unfortunately, canceling a card may be the only option for those spenders who just can't control their charging habits. You can maintain your debt, but shouldn't add any more to it through purchases. To help you do this, transfer your balances to one card and cancel all the rest.

5. Sidestep purchase requirements

Some credit cards may require you to make purchases with their card in order to maintain debt with a very low interest rate. Discover Card has recently been offering 0% interest for the life of your loan (balance transfer or otherwise) as long as you make a purchase within each billing period.

With this gimmick, the credit card companies are at it again. Most cards require you to pay off your lower interest rates before you can pay down the debt at a higher APR. That means you'll be paying high interest rates as long as you have the card despite the 0% deal on a portion of your loan. If you use the same card as your primary credit card for purchases, you could be back where you started with high interest payments sooner than later. After a few months with this scheme, you could be paying a ton in finance charges for the purchases you make, even if you have a low APR on your original balance.

There are some nice things in the fine print, however, and with deals like this, they usually only require one or two payments a month to maintain the offer. That could be a lot when you're buying yachts or alligators with your card, but if you buy a pack of gum at the grocery store, you're only adding 50 cents a purchase. High interest on that may reach a penny or two for the life of the loan.

Additionally, with the advent of online payments, one can really start taking advantage of these offers. My brother and I have this aforementioned deal on a couple of cards and we make a donation in the amount of one cent with each card every month to RenascentCulture. com, a cultural project of ours. The payment is secure through Paypal, so we don't need to worry about giving out our credit card information, unfortunately however, Paypal does eat the penny donation, as a service charge.

6. Cash the $15 check for credit protector

Every once in a while, you may receive a check in the mail for $9.99 or $15—not a loan, free money. At first glace, you may think that it was awful nice of someone to just give you money. But of course there's a catch. When you cash the check or deposit it, you will automatically be enrolled in a credit protection offer, in which they will charge you a percentage of your credit balance and a monthly fee in exchange for their service (it's basically insurance).

I don't recommend this program because it adds to your debt with just a small chance of benefit to you, but you could possibly use this gimmick to your advantage. This is because the $15 check is real money and it's yours if you cash it. It could give you an entrée at a restaurant or a couple pairs of nice socks, and all you have to do is cash the check. But, if you do, you must remember to call the company and cancel the protection service once you receive the membership information. If you neglect this small step, you'll be paying upwards of $30 a month for a service you probably won't need.

The offer will include a number that you can call to cancel. Sometimes it is on the check itself, so write it down before banking it. The call to cancel may take about 5 minutes, but it's mindless communication and you can do it while you pay bills or browse the Internet for other great credit card deals.

The conversation may go something like this:

"Hi welcome to Protektor Kredit Company, how can I help you?"

"I'd like to cancel."

"Are you sure? We really value you as a customer."

"Yes, I'm sure."

"Really?"

"Yes."

"Really, really?"

"Yes."

"Really, really, really??"

"Yes."

"Is that your final answer?"

"Yes."

"Okay, can I have your membership number?"

And so on. The customer service reps will try to keep your business, but if you are terse and certain about your decision, they will cancel your membership.

You may not be interested in dealing with people like this, but it is well worth it. It might take up to 5 minutes to complete this call and so that's $15 in 5 minutes or $180 an hour. If you're not making $180 dollars an hour (and who is?), it is worth it. You must make sure you cancel before the free month expires, though.

When you do call to cancel, you may receive additional benefits to continue your free trial. The mentality of the protector company is maybe they can get you to forget about canceling their service next month if it didn't work this time. This happened to me when I cancelled a membership to a similar program (but for auto protection) before the free trial ended. I called to cancel and the customer service rep explained that they were better than the competition because they gave their customers a year of free oil changes. I replied that I hadn't received any free oil change certificates, which prompted the rep to offer to send me those oil change certificates and extend the free trial another month. I accepted and made a note to cancel one month later.

Sometimes, these programs sign you up for a year's membership when the trial month ends, and that could end up costing over $100. Other programs don't offer a free trial period, which is something to be weary of. If you cash a check for a paid service, it's just a discount for their service, not free money—make sure it comes with a free trial.

7. Utilize cash-back offers

Some credit card companies will offer you a cash-back award for purchases—take advantage of this! A friend of mine received an offer at one point basically because he hadn't used the card in some time. They offered him an instant $5 cash-back reward for each of the first three purchases he made. The card company's goal in this was to get him to dust off his card and start swiping it wherever he went because they make a certain percentage on every transaction. Even if he pays off his balance every month to avoid finance charges, the card still makes money off his purchases. Of course, *he* wouldn't be paying the credit card any more money with each transaction directly, but the merchant would be, and that usually comes back to the consumer through higher prices.

Five dollars isn't much of a return when you're paying 50 dollars for your groceries, but if you make three payments of $.01 in the manner explained before, the $15 you make is like free money.

8. Rewards City

"I can receive a brand new Huffy bicycle and all I need to spend on a credit card is $25,000?!" You may be a little skeptical of rewards and frequent flyer miles earned through credit cards. You may need to spend the equivalent of the price of a small airplane to accrue any flight at all, and that seems like a hefty goal if that's the only reason you're using the card. But if you can pay phone bills and the like with your credit card, and you use it for all of your normal purchases, those rewards limits are more attainable than you may think especially if you can get extra miles for things that you already purchase. Additionally, the rewards are often pretty nice.

After my United Visa upgraded me to the miles card equivalent of box seats (no annual fee), I started looking into all the offers they had for people like me. I was shocked to find that I could earn miles on every dollar I spent and bonus miles on things that I was paying for already. I concluded that I could have been taking advantage of these offers for a while and proceeded to kick myself thoroughly. Until that point, I had been using a debit card to pay for everything, which was good for my accounting, but not good for taking advantage of the people who were trying to take advantage of me. I spent a lot of money on various things each month, from computers to corn and everything in between, and those monetary transactions weren't benefiting me in any way. I figured that I could have earned at least a couple roundtrip tickets to Hawai'i and maybe a cruise or two with all the dollars I've spent on everyday stuff. Sure, some of the rewards that you can get are unwanted (cheese of the month club or a 1,000-pack of sporks), but most rewards cards' networks are so extensive, they're bound to have something you want. If the alternative is no benefit, aren't you gaining at least something by participating in the rewards program?

A friend of mine recently received an offer to transfer balances to her Bank of America rewards card without a transfer fee and get a reward point for every $100 transferred (a reward point was worth a $1 payout or a fraction of a gift certificate). The interest rate on her reward card was a few points lower than her other card, so she didn't blink and transferred the entire debt, making the equivalent of $90.

In another example, another friend really made out well. This example incorporates a few concepts in this book that we will discuss later in addition to rewards cards and is so good sometimes I can't believe it happened. Here's how it came together:

One day when my friend was preparing to go on a trip to Los Angeles, he was looking online for a hotel room. He didn't have any place in particular he wanted to stay, so he looked at the usual online travel sites for the best deal (flexibility has its rewards when it comes to Ad-in). While he was on the Expedia.com website, he noticed that they were offering a $150 gift certificate for every purchase being made during a special offer.

He found a decent four-star hotel (my friend won't stay at a hotel with fewer than four stars) in the heart of the city with a pretty good rate of $150 a night. He noticed that the hotel was one he had stayed at before in another city, so he signed up for a frequent stay program (similar to the frequent flyer program). With the program, he would earn a free night's stay after purchasing four nights. Since this stay would be four nights, he would earn a free night with the program. The hotel was also associated with American Airlines and gave him AAdvantage miles in addition to his hotel reward.

He used his rewards credit card, which gave him a point for every dollar spent and double points if he bought from an affiliated merchant. Expedia.com was an affiliated merchant, so he earned double points on this purchase on his credit card.

After typing and clicking a little while to set up his accounts, my friend made the purchase. When it was all said and done this is what he spent and earned:

Expenses
4 nights at the four-star The Tower (Loews) Beverly Hills at $150/night: $600

Rewards
Expedia.com coupon: $150 off the next purchase
Loews rewards: 1 free night ($150+)
AAdvantage miles: 600
ThankYouRewards (credit card) points: 1,200

With one purchase, he earned rewards at the hotel where he was staying, the online travel agency, the airline he used to fly there, and the credit card he used to make the purchase. Altogether, he saved about $350 on future purchases by purchasing a hotel stay that was fairly priced in the first place.

I've recently had success with rewards cards as well, but not with spending on them, just signing up. I applied for a card that was affiliated with my United Airlines frequent flyer program and got a free flight when I used my card for the first time. Of course they expected me to keep using the card so that they could make money, but I swiftly cut up the card after flying to Seattle to visit my sister. They had a $60 annual fee for the card, which I paid, but all things considered, that was an inexpensive flight to Seattle. Consequently, when I called to cancel the card as the annual fee was going to renew, an offer for the same card with the same benefits but with no annual fee was miraculously uncovered and offered. I currently use this Platinum version of the card for most of my purchases now.

Some cards will give you rewards, like a free flight, just for signing up *and* waive the annual fee for the first year. I believe the technical term for that in the financial industry is a "no-brainer".

9. Make money off of the credit card companies

Andrew Kahr is known as the innovator of the credit card industry. His clients, financial institutions like Bank One, Schwab One, and CMA, have paid him to come up with new ways to take advantage of their credit card consumers. Since Kahr has been at it, he has changed the industry dramatically to favor his clients.

When Mr. Kahr entered the industry, lenders were requiring their customers to pay a standard minimum payment of 5% each month. Kahr suggested that consumers would be more willing to spend more and increase their debt if their monthly payment was lower. Most consumers feel that they are being prudent financially when they only have to pay $40 on a $2,000 debt instead of $100. This seems like a big difference, and it is. Customers with plans like these will end up spending twice the original loan amount by paying just the minimum, but they continue to do it, and they feel good about it. This was one of the consumer behaviors that Kahr was in tune with and was able to exploit for the benefit of credit card companies.

Years ago, Kahr also encouraged one of his clients to start doing business with people in other states so that they could take advantage of the usury laws of certain states. As described above, states like South Dakota and Delaware allow companies to charge whatever interest they choose to people even if they live in other states like New York. But most companies didn't understand the process or thought it was illegal, according to Kahr. It was innovators like Andrew Kahr that most credit companies have to thank for their bulging wallets.

Another innovation Kahr implemented was the 0% short-term rate. He convinced one of his clients to provide loans with no interest rate to customers, new and old, on purchases and balance transfers for a short time only. In his plan, after the designated trial ended, the rate would return to the normal rate.

This proved to be a great way for banks to attract new customers and to get more debt transferred from another financial institution. Once all of this debt was built up in the new account, the interest rate would jump, and the company would begin to see major profits. It is a risk for the credit card company to do this, however, and the fact that they do it proves that the credit card business is dog-eat-dog. "This is an example of how competitive the industry is, particularly in the prime card sector right now," Kahr explained, "that banks are willing to make deals with consumers that in some instances they require as long as two or three years to pass before they can get back what they have invested in terms of lending money at no interest and so forth."

Most of us can take advantage of this competition and actually make money off of the credit cards. The process is simple, though it may require some diligence on the part of you, the borrower. If you take the money that lenders are willing to loan to you for free and put it in a money market or other investment, you can stand to gain a considerable amount of money, all at the expense of the credit card company.

I first got the idea to do this when I received an offer for a 0% promotional APR for an entire year on a Bank of America card that I already had. They gave me convenience checks that had no fee or finance charge associated with them, and I could cash them like any normal check or deposit them in my bank account. In other words, I wasn't forced to transfer a balance from another credit card to take advantage of the nonexistent APR.

I deposited the money in my checking account, fought the urge to go on a shopping spree for large appliances and other things I didn't need, and bought some stocks with the money. The stock rose over the next several months, giving me a return on my investment, and when the trial period was over, I sold the stock, transferred the money back to my bank account, paid off the credit card, and pocketed the gains.

I can't recommend purchasing stocks for everyone since they are so risky—depending on the market, you could lose your whole investment (I've had my share of losses to be sure). One can buy into a mutual fund or other more reliable investment to reduce the risk or invest in an interest-earning savings account for even less risk. Though I put it in a fairly stable stock, the risk was still there. Luckily, I did end up coming out a little ahead with this venture, and there were other benefits that opened the door to a number of other opportunities.

One of the major benefits of this technique is that it forces you to save and invest money. Although the credit card interest rate is at 0%, the company still requires you to make a minimum payment each month, so you're still putting forth some capital. The difference is that all of that payment goes to the principle of your loan, not the interest.

Let's assume that the minimum payment for the $5,000 was $100 a month to make it simple. At the end of the year, you would have paid down $1,200 of the loan, which means, at the end of the year, you would only have to pay the card company $3,800 to pay off the balance. Since the average increase of the stock market of the last few decades is around 10%, you would probably be able to sell your stock at around $5,500. This would give you a net of $1,700 at the end of the year, a third of which was thanks to that kind credit card company that lent you the money.

Other ways that you can invest this money are CDs, which are guaranteed money, though they have a small return; money market funds, which return a bit more interest and are fairly stable; and mutual funds, which are slightly less risky than stocks and may cost you maintenance fees.

Detractors would say to just deposit $100 a month in a money market account and earn the interest that way. This is prudent advice. However, since the total amount is just a fraction of what it would be if you used the bank's money, the return on your investment would be equally small. With the 0% loan, you can gain leverage and earn much more than you would with just your savings.

It is not advised to invest loaned money in your IRA or other retirement accounts, or in investments that you cannot liquidate immediately. This Ad-In technique requires you to sell your assets at the end of the promotional period and pay off the remaining debt so that you don't incur any fees or finance charges. If you invest this loan into a retirement account, you won't be able to withdraw before you're 59-and-a-half years of age without a steep penalty, essentially defeating the purpose.

There is the option of transferring your balance at the end of the promotional period, which I did, to another credit card offering 0% APR for another year. The balance was transferred to this other card, again with no fee associated, for twelve more months. The first card offered another convenience check with the same offer, so I took advantage of that one as well.

On another occasion, I received an offer for a 0% rate on only balance transfers, but I didn't have any balance to transfer that wasn't already at 0%. I couldn't take advantage of the offer because I couldn't access the money they were willing to loan me. However, another card had mailed me convenience checks that would have incurred a 3.99% APR, and I could easily access that money by depositing it into my checking account, so I cashed a convenience check and immediately transferred the balance to the 0% card. There are countless ways to finagle these offers, but the value is there and it's worth taking advantage of.

You can see how this technique could amass a large amount of debt and get out of hand in no time. It is important to keep track of each card and when the promotional trials for each card end. Write it down or, if you have access to a database program, compile a spreadsheet of the cards you have, their balances, their APRs, and when the introductory period ends.

If you don't keep track, you could be stuck with a large finance charge after the rates return to normal, as happened to a friend of mine who attempted this. It ended up costing him over $140 in finance charges because he forgot when the promotional rate was going to end. Fortunately, he had made enough money in the sale of his stock positions to cover this loss. But, to be sure, it made the process bittersweet.

When done correctly, this technique can make you a substantial amount of money. I bought a small position of the search engine Google's stock right after its initial public offering (IPO) and paid $110 per share. I sold the stock when it was at $180 a share and made a nice profit. Of course, I've been kicking myself ever since as I watch the value climb to $400 and more per share. A $5,000 investment in Google right after the IPO would have returned $20,000 in a little over a year.

Of course, stocks like Google don't come around all the time, and even with stocks like Google, the increasing value isn't guaranteed, as seen in the 25% drop in the beginning of 2006. The stock market is a risky place to invest money, especially if the money isn't yours. There are other options, however, with this technique. If you put the $5,000 in a CD, you could end up with a guaranteed $250 at the end of the year. It may not seem like a lot, but it could certainly help with expenses around the holidays, for instance. Or, you could make a nice donation to your favorite charity at the expense of your friendly bank.

Things to avoid

Debt consolidation companies: it may sound nice to have all your debt in one nice monthly payment, but if they don't offer a great interest rate (3% or lower), they are just taking advantage of you. If you receive an offer from one of these companies and want to look into it, make sure of a few things:

1. They are offering a fixed interest rate that is better than what you are paying currently.
2. There is no transfer or consolidation fee. They're going to be making lots of money on you through interest; there should be no up-front fees.
3. There isn't a prepayment or cancellation fee. Some companies will charge you if you do not keep paying for years on end.

There are a number of legitimate non-profit sources that provide debt management. Some universities, military bases, credit unions, housing authorities, and branches of the U.S. Cooperative Extension Service offer counseling, workshops, and free information packages to people in debt trouble. You may feel more comfortable seeking out a company that is affiliated with a business you know, like your bank, as opposed to working with a company that has sent you a cheap flyer in the mail.

Franklin Says:

"All mankind is divided into three classes: those that are immovable, those that are movable, and those that move."

The Culprit: credit card companies

The Target: consumerism, laziness, forgetfulness, greed

Ad-In requires: diligence to monitor separate credit cards, investment skills

What Ben Earned:
• lowered APR (US Average)	$2,875.98
• credit protector enrollment	$15
• free oil changes	$75
• instant cash-back for purchases	$14.97
• rewards	$985
• investments from 0% interest card	$500
Total	$4,815.95

Part Three

Making Money on Money

"I believe that banking institutions are more dangerous to our liberties than standing armies. If the American people ever allow private banks to control the issue of their currency, first by inflation, then by deflation, the banks and corporations that will grow up around [the banks] will deprive the people of all property until their children wake-up homeless on the continent their fathers conquered. "

- Thomas Jefferson

"A bank is a place that will lend you money if you can prove that you don't need it."

-Bob Hope

Credit cards are just one aspect of the ever-opportunistic banking industry. Banks can make money on just about everything having to do with money. When they give you money in the form of a secure loan, for instance, they make money on the interest that you pay them. When *you* give *them* money and they pay you interest, as in the case of a Certificate of Deposit, they still make money because they turn around and invest your money and get a larger return on it than they give you. Banks have it down when it comes to earning money on money.

It may seem unfair or immoral the way that banks make money on such a simple thing as money. Some may say, "Why should a bank be able to take 80% of my mortgage payment every month when they're not doing anything really?" Or, "I'm letting them use the money in my checking account, why does it cost for me to take money out?"

The arguments against banks and their seemingly voracious appetites for your money are unending and valid. It does seem unfair that many banks charge their customers to talk to a human teller. It does seem awfully greedy that banks charge, say, an 8% interest rate on a mortgage loan, but give only 5% interest on the best Certificate of Deposit.

It can safely be said that banks are not in the business to make the *customer* wealthy; they're in it to make themselves rich. But however unfair it may seem to you, imagine what life would be like without banks? We would be restricted to hoarding our earnings under our mattresses, which would be easy targets for burglars; we would have to keep ridiculous amounts of cash on hand to pay for everything because we wouldn't be able to conveniently write checks; and we would have to wait an eternity to buy anything substantial, like a house or a car, because we couldn't take out hefty loans.

Would you like it if the only way to be able to buy a house was to fork over the $400,000 on the spot? Of course you wouldn't. Some people can do that, but I haven't met anyone recently who's that comfortable monetarily. Banks allow us to store our savings, transport money conveniently, and use a lot of money that's not ours to buy things we couldn't otherwise afford. The last benefit can have adverse effects on personal finance if not properly handled (as seen in the last section), but overall, these capabilities are extremely beneficial to us and to our economy. Though some economists may argue that banks just increase the rate of inflation, the institutions are invaluable to our economy and standard of living.

So, banks do offer a lot of great services and products, and they contribute positively to the economy. Altogether, the product banks offer is the *power of wealth*. Chase Manhattan Bank is the leading bank with regard to assets. It has over $365 billion (yes, that's a 'b'), almost twenty percent more than number two in the industry, Citicorp. There were over 7,500 national banks reporting to the Federal Deposit Insurance Corporation (the organization that protects up to $100,000 of your deposits at your bank) in 2005, and about half of the institutions claimed assets greater than $100 million.

You don't have to be a mathematician to realize that banks have a lot of wealth, something that the author and probably the readers of this book lack. Whenever someone has a product that another person wants, there is supply and demand, and the laws of economics take over.

Like any product, whether it is a bottle of orange juice you buy at the store or a new car, the bank's product is worth something to us consumers. Since it's worth something to us, it is logical that we pay something in exchange for it. No one will protest paying a fair amount for something even if it is an abstract product like a loan or the convenience of writing a check.

But since a bank's products are abstract, consumers can lose sight of what they're actually paying. The cost is distributed over a long period of time or separated into several different categories that reach the consumer at different times through different avenues. The bank might take advantage of the natural obscurity of the price to fool the consumer into paying more than is fair. Indeed, the bank might multiply the layers of abstraction to get the most from the customer. This is the essence of taking advantage of the consumer and must be defeated.

A few years ago, I signed up for a checking account at Bank of America. The banker was nice and helped me pick out a certain account that fit my potential banking behavior. After a few times depositing money at the human teller, she explained that I was being charged every time I spoke to a teller. The ATM was free to use, but talking with humans cost two bucks. I shrugged it off and started using the ATM. I would miss the personal interaction, but it was more convenient to just use the drive-through ATM anyway, so I complied.

The bank did not charge me a monthly fee for the account, and I was pleased with that, though I later found out that the account *did* incur a monthly fee that was being waived because I was utilizing direct deposit. I didn't know about the fee until I stopped using direct deposit and noticed a $5 charge on my statement every month.

After customer service explained that it was a "maintenance fee". I asked if my account had structural damage or needed to be cleaned with a mop. He didn't appreciate my attempt at humor and refused to refund all of the $5 fees over the last few months for which I hadn't been auditing my statements.

I didn't think that was a very nice thing to do, so I went in to the local branch to cancel my accounts. The banker who helped me was not as friendly as the one who signed me up and was not impressed when I told her that I was leaving because of all the ridiculous fees. I had to ask her if there was a fee for talking to her to close my account. She looked as if the answer was obvious, "*No.*" Oh, of course not.

She asked me if I wanted cash for the money that I was withdrawing from my accounts instead of a check and I told her yes. Just then, she crumpled the check she was filling out and started again explaining, "There's a $5 check-cashing fee . . ."

Yes, they do get fairly carried away with their fees at banks. The fees mentioned above, along with overdraft fees and low-balance fees and the like are so menacing it's a wonder why we use banks at all. It seems like we spend more money at banks than we actually deposit.

Thank God that there is competition in the banking industry, and we aren't forced to deal with one bank's controlling policies. There are so many banks—7,549 national banks to be exact—that if you don't like how one is treating you, you can usually find another with similar positive qualities without all the negative qualities. After I cancelled my account with Bank of America, I walked across the parking lot to the Washington Mutual and deposited my cash into a new account with no monthly fees. Also, it's possible that just threatening to leave for another bank will instigate better and more cost-efficient service. A friend of mine had a checking account at Bank of America, and she had the monthly fee waved after she told them she wanted to close the account. It's funny how that works, huh?

With mergers and buyouts, the number of banks is actually decreasing; the peak was in 1984 when there were over 14,800. However, there are still enough out there, and it's still a profitable enough industry to ensure a great deal of competition. For every two banks that tire their customers with endless lists of fees, there is a smart upstart that will pull in customers by offering fee-less banking. Washington Mutual is an example of this and CitiBank has launched a program called Simplicity that similarly reduces fees.

10. Find banks that are willing to pay you to do business

Banks can make money on just about every aspect of the capital trade, and, as seen with the numbers above, they're doing quite well at it. ATM fees alone in 2005 netted over $2 billion for banks. But banks need customers to make all their money, and, when banks gain a customer, it tends to be for an extended period of time, usually more than a few years and sometimes an entire life (the average is about seven years per customer). That's why many banks are willing to give you nice offers to get you to do business with them.

Research in 2005 showed that most customers who leave their banks do so because of moving or death. The small minority (just 2%) leaves for other reasons, such as the customer dissatisfaction mentioned above.

Banks are still trying very hard to reduce the latter; they're redesigning banks to make them friendlier and more appealing, they're extending their hours to fit better with the schedules of everyday customers, and they're spending more on advertising. They're doing all this for one reason: you are profitable!

Just a few years ago, a normal checking account holder at a bank, let's say with an average of $1,200 in his account, actually cost a bank to maintain. Now, with better technology, even marginal-balance checking customers are profitable. When you tack on the income that banks receive from fees on most customers, they're doing very well on even customers with small balances.

So, since you're giving something to them (money that they can invest with), why not make them give something to you? It's most likely that there are a number of bank branches within a close proximity to where you live, and most may offer some sort of free checking account. It's your job to find one with a great offer to open an account and close out your previous account.

Citibank has been taking noticeable steps to attract new customers, offering as much as $220 in gifts. This total usually requires you to open a checking account with a certain amount, a savings account with a minimum balance, and perhaps sign up with direct deposit, but if you can meet those requirements, $220 is certainly worth the move.

They also offered a free iPod Nano when applying for a home equity line of credit in mid-2006. While the $199 impossibly-small music player might not seem like enough of an incentive to sign up for a home equity line of credit and to tie up your equity, it may help to know that it won't cost you in time or effort or reflect negatively on your credit. On the offer, there were no application fees, no points, no closing costs, and no interest payments on the line of credit until you made a purchase. And if you're very strange and don't want an iPod Nano for some reason, you can always find an eager buyer on eBay that will give you real money for it.

With this deal, you would incur penalty fees for closing the account prematurely, and the APR isn't much to write home about (prime minus 0.25%). Realistically, though, the gift would be yours for free without any obligation. If you're in the market for loans of this nature, you should know that the company giving you the offer stands to make a lot of money on your potential loan, and an iPod Nano is the least the creditor should offer.

Commerce Bank of New Jersey likes to promote its more traditional new-customer gifts, like toasters and waffle makers. The bank is bringing in new customers at a whopping rate, and they can thank George Foreman for it. The bank gave away 800 Foreman Grills to new customers in the first few months of its existence in Washington, D.C.

There might be a bit of hassle moving your accounts to a new bank, including a longer wait period for cleared funds, which is normal for new customers, but all in all it may be well worth the 20 minutes it takes to talk to a banker to save all the money you may pay in fees every month. And you might get a nice new iPod or Foreman Grill in the process.

11. Utilize online bill pay

Online bill pay is another service that banks may give you a gift or monetary compensation for using. When I was with Bank of America, they were offering $5 to everyone who signed up for the program. It's understandable, too, that banks would want you to use this service. Aside from causing the customer to associate more closely with the bank and to visit its website more often (which is always good for any company), there are a number of reasons why the banks want customers to use online bill pay.

Catherine Graeber of Forrester Research says about bill pay customers that smart banks, "now understand the impact these customers have on the bottom line. These customers buy more products, do more self-service and have higher retention rates." When I made my switch to a new bank, the worst part about it was going from a comfortable setup, where I paid all my bills to a blank slate. My new bank offered online bill pay, but the idea of transferring all the payee information over was a little daunting. In this respect, I can certainly understand why the retention rate for customers who use online bill pay is higher.

Major banks are starting to realize the value of online bill pay as a tool to foster better business relationships with their customers. That's mainly why they have eliminated the monthly fees that were common with this tool after its inception.

Besides taking advantage of the deals your bank may offer you to start online bill pay, you should take advantage of the tool based on its merits alone. Online bill pay allows you to access your accounts and your bills all in the same place, making accounting more efficient, and it alleviates you from the responsibility and hassle of physical checks, envelopes, and stamps. I'm not an accountant at heart or anything, but I actually find it rather fun to pay bills online.

To be sure, the banks are taking advantage of their online bill pay customers—when the majority of these transactions go completely electronic, the banks will be saving millions—but that doesn't mean that you won't be able to take advantage of them in return.

Online security shouldn't be a reason to deter you either; most bank websites offering bill pay are encoded and secure. On the contrary, paying bills online reduces the number of people who handle your check as it makes its way through the channels to its destination. 27 million of the total 75 million online households already use bill pay in one form or the other. If you value convenience, perhaps you should use the tool too.

12. Try credit unions

If you are completely disillusioned by the entire banking process, it's understandable. Fees and low payment interest on your deposits and high rates on loans will catch the ire of any reasonable customer. Luckily, there are other options.

Credit unions, which are community-based, non-profit organizations, may be your answer to lower fees and better returns on your deposits. Credit unions are owned and operated by the members of the union, who are also shareholders. They are usually customers of the union as well, a situation that promotes less cutthroat interest rates and traditionally better service.

Since credit unions are non-profit, their goal isn't to make money on you. Instead, the money that those organizations take in is redistributed in the form of higher interest rates for savings. You can take advantage of the better rates of credit unions, which are taking advantage of you to increase their membership. The more members they have, the more of an edge they have over banks.

At the beginning of February 2006, the edge was over a full percentage point more on Certificates of Deposit and more than a full percentage point less on $30,000 HELOC loans.

There are major drawbacks with credit unions, however. Since the unions are localized, they usually don't have convenient ATMs on the corner of every block in your city next to each Starbucks shop. If you need a branch in every other major city, you may want to stick with one of the larger banks. Technology is also an aspect in which credit unions lag in the competition with banks. The lack of fees and good rates may be more important than all of that, however, so credit unions may be the ideal situation for you.

While banks can help you make money on your money, the best way to do this has to do with homeownership, which will be explained further in the next chapter.

Franklin Says:
"Beware of little expenses. A small leak will sink a great ship. "

The Culprit: banks

The Target: abstract nature of currency, personal routine

Ad-In requires: time and effort to change banks

What Ben Earned:
- no monthly check account fee (annual) $60
- online bill pay start-up reward $5
- savings on $30,000 HELOC loan $300
- loan sign-up bonus $199

Total $554

Part Four

The Two Most Expensive Purchases of Your Life

"A person who can acquire no property, can have no other interest but to eat as much, and to labour as little as possible. Whatever work he does beyond what is sufficient to purchase his own maintenance can be squeezed out of him by violence only, and not by any interest of his own."

Adam Smith

Are you impressed yet?! At this point, if you have done all of the techniques described to take back the advantage from the scoundrel credit card companies and banks, you should have saved or made a couple thousand dollars. Wow, maybe I should consider raising the cost of this book. Just kidding. It's NOT all about the Benjamins, despite what P. Diddy has been known for saying (for those readers who aren't tight with the rapper extraordinaire, Benjamins are $100 bills). There are other reasons for producing this book, in fact my main goal is social and financial justice, and that happens when more people begin to take the advantage back from the major financial institutions. The more people who practice Ad-in, the more justice there will be in the market economy, and that's the real goal. So if you've learned some great tips that you have made money on, please feel free to spread the word!

There is a chance that you're one of the 12 adults in the Western world who hasn't dealt with banks or credit cards in your life, in which case the previous two sections haven't benefited you. If that's the case, I'd like to make it up to you. I'd like to describe Ad-in techniques for two financial decisions that almost everyone ends up making at some point in their lives. If, after this chapter, you still haven't found anything that applies to your financial life, I'll be glad to give you a full refund. Then you can go back to roaming the world like a hunter/gatherer. In this chapter, I will describe the automobile and housing institutions, potentially representing two of the most important financial decisions you can make.

While the Certificates of Deposit and savings accounts mentioned in the last chapter are solid ways to make your money work for you, they don't quite have the allure of other sound investments. This might be because of the relatively low interest rates that those types of deposits carry. Money markets are similarly unsubstantial with regard to their return on investment, though they usually return a bit more. The main benefit of those investment paths is the lack of risk.

If you're willing to accept a bit more risk, there are a number of sound investments that you can explore for greater return.

While automobiles are not usually seen as investments, a car is the most significant purchase that the typical person can make, apart from a house, and it is important that the buyer gets it right. When attempting to take advantage of the automobile sale situation, there are a number of factors to be concerned with, all of which can be illustrated when describing the car-buying habits of the typical American millionaire.

Truly wealthy people (those with assets in excess of $1 million) have distinct habits that are easy to pick out and contrast against those who are not wealthy. It may be helpful to emulate those habits as they most likely have contributed to their wealth.

13. Ownership has its privileges

American millionaires *buy* their cars as opposed to leasing them. Does this sound counterintuitive to you? It may seem reasonable to think of a millionaire as the type of person who would *lease* a car and exchange it for another new one in a year or two so as to maintain fresh, stylish transportation, but this is not the case. A study of millionaires done by Thomas J. Stanley and William D. Danko concluded that about 81% of the millionaires in America purchased their automobiles.

The goal for the rest of us *thousandaires* may be then to try and emulate their behavior in order to upgrade to millionaire status. It would behoove us to imitate the habits that help those millionaires get to their monetary status, but what if buying cars isn't a habit that helped them become millionaires? What if millionaires just bought their cars instead of leasing simply because they could? After all, millionaires have the ability to buy cars on the spot without taking out loans, which ends up costing them less in the long run. Even if a millionaire didn't have enough pocket change to buy his or her car on the spot, the cost would still not be burdensome. A $30,000 car is less than 1% of the average millionaire's total net worth. In this regard, a millionaire buying a car is like a book author buying a really nice tire. *One* tire. Evidently, though, it appears that wealthy people buy their cars (and hold on to them for long periods) because doping so pays off in the long run.

Still, millionaires probably know something about car shopping that non-millionaires like us could learn. Millionaires usually take advantage of a market that rewards patience. Edmunds.com conducted a study to compare the total cost of a new $20,000 car including car loan, gas, insurance, maintenance, and DMV fees when purchasing versus leasing the same car. The study revealed that the first year cost of leasing was cheaper ($6,600 versus $11,500), but the five-year total was about the same for the two cars ($32,000). Thereafter, it paid to own, not only because the leased car was worth nothing to the driver after the lease ended, but also because the lease price would likely stay the same or increase, while a car loan payment would decrease.

So, according to this study, it takes about 5 years for a purchase to start paying off with regard to autos. Some people appreciate the emotional effect of having a new car too much to have to endure one car for that long, but owning a car does pay off in the long run. Three million millionaires must know something that people who lease do not.

14. Buy per pound

Envision a lineup of automobiles that Joe Millionaire is considering buying. I'd like you to try to guess the car that he is most likely to purchase. In the lineup, we have a Ferrari F40, a Lexus SC 430 convertible, a Honda Accord, a Ford F150 pickup, and a Mercedes S Class. Can you guess which car our millionaire friend would be most inclined to buy? Here's a hint: it's also the most popular car for the non-millionaires too.

It turns out that the Ford F150 is the most popular model that American millionaires buy. The survey by Stanley and Danko mentioned above noted that wealthy people tend to purchase their motor vehicles by the pound. Millionaires' cars cost around $7 per pound, while a Mercedes Benz 500 SL costs around $22 per pound. The Ferrari is an incomprehensible $175 per pound.

This doesn't mean that millionaires are necessarily cheap when it comes to cars, just that they are into reliability and value over appearance. If style and status don't appeal to you, you can take advantage of the price per pound of a car and not the flashy looks.

15. Let someone else pay for your down payment

The minute someone drives their brand new car off the lot, it loses an average of 20% of its value. It's a wonder, then, why most people are ecstatic and gleaming with joy at that same time. They just bought something that is now instantly worth $4,200 less, yet they are happy. It is unclear whether that ubiquitous new car scent has anything to do with this bizarre behavior.

It's true that there is nothing like driving a new automobile, and to some people, that experience is worth that 20% loss of value. Most people, however, would choose to avoid such a drop in the value of one of their possessions if they were aware of this figure.

I recently looked up a 2006 Mercedes C Class on Cars.com to see what was available. To buy that specific model new, you would have to come up with $36,575. From the same website, I looked up the exact same car on the pre-owned search. Besides some used cars that were more expensive than the new car, there was an obvious trend. The majority of the used 2006 Mercedes C Class cars were about 15-25% cheaper than the brand new one. There were a couple cars with less than 50 miles on the odometer that were going for $7,000 less than the brand new car.

There is a risk of buying a lemon with a car that sells for 80% of the cost of a new car when it only has 34 miles on it, but with online resources (all the major websites have certified links to research the history of any car) the car's condition is easy to research. In addition, if you purchase the car through the dealer an extended warranty is usually available.

Of the 2005 models of the same car, the average was about $27,000. These cars are available because of those who lease brand new cars for $600 a month on a one-year contract. You can take advantage of people and their proclivity to buy new cars and take their 12-month-old Mercedes off their hands with a nice 27% deduction off the original sticker price. In addition, studies have shown that the new car scent lasts up to two years, so you won't even have to miss out on that!

16. Sell your car in the country (and buy in the city)

While the cost of living in rural areas is generally lower than in urban areas, you can usually fetch a higher price for your automobile when you sell it in the country. If you have ever tried to find the value of your car on an online car market, you may have wondered why they ask you for your zip code before the process. They're asking because the same motor vehicle is worth more in rural areas where the population is lower and the competition for used cars is minimal.

On the Kelley Blue Book website, the value of a 2000 Acura Integra sedan in excellent condition is worth $9,270 in Sheridan, Indiana. In the generally more expensive New York City, the same exact car with the same exact condition and mileage would be sold for $9,020. This is true for most any car—try it yourself. It's worthwhile to note the disparity. One could purchase an entire apartment complex in Sheridan, Indiana, for the amount of money one could buy a 500-square-foot apartment in New York City, but *cars*, for some reason, are more expensive in Sheridan.

Though it might not make sense, the country car discount does exist. If you can, take advantage of the population and competition difference by purchasing your automobile in the city and selling it in the country.

17. Let the bank make money for you on a house with leverage

The largest purchase of many people's lives, beating out that of an automobile, is that of a home. While owning a car as opposed to leasing one is a smart move because it tends to save money in the long run, buying a home instead of renting not only saves the buyer money in the long-run, it actually earns the buyer money. There are a number of benefits to owning a home that I'm sure everyone has heard: tax deductions, a more stable budget, and gaining equity. But, for many, the idea of purchasing a home may seem daunting and unrealistic.

At the time of this writing, real estate prices in California are just coming down from all-time highs. The median sale price of an existing home was about $550,000. In a nice area in one of the larger cities, one could look to spend that much on a one-bedroom condo and to many people, that sounds ridiculously high, especially with all the talk of a 'housing bubble' threatening to burst.

While no one can predict the future, it's hard to imagine home prices going up much more than they have in the past decade, but people have been saying this since the housing prices were half of what they are now. Demand for housing continues to increase with the population, so housing prices will likely follow. As one economist has said, "God keeps making people, but he's done making more land."

If there is a bubble, and housing prices are overpriced, it would be a great opportunity to start looking for a place in the area that you are interested in (you can make a *low-ball* offer without getting laughed out of the city). If you plan on staying in your home for at least five years, there's very little chance that you will lose money in equity on your house. Most likely, you will gain a substantial amount on your investment (the average annual appreciation for homes recently is 6%).

The main reason that you can make a substantial amount on real estate can be found in the vital concept of leverage. Leverage is the use of financial instruments (e.g. a loan) to increase the potential return of an investment. It can be summarized as follows:

Let's say that you wanted to buy 10 shares of a stock, which in total would cost you $100. If you were to leverage another $20, that is, to take a loan out for that much more and invest that additional amount with your original $100, you would have $120 invested and you would be able retain all of the return on investment. Let's say the stock price doubled in 5 years. You would have stock worth $240 (as opposed to $200 without the loan). You would, of course have to pay for the interest on your loan, but the financial institution has no claim on the amount that you have gained on your investment.

The benefit of purchasing a *house* with leverage (or a loan) is that you can borrow on a significantly higher amount than with other investments. For instance, a bank is almost eager to give a home loan of 80% to someone with a decent credit rating, but a loan for stocks is much more risky, so financial institutions often aren't willing to go over 33% of the total value. In other words, a broker might lend you 50% of your equity to buy additional stocks, but a bank may lend you 400% of your investment to purchase a house.

Since real estate is such a sound purchase, banks can do this and still make money. They want to know that the borrower will pay their interest every month, but besides that, they don't really care about what happens to the value of the house. It could triple in value and the bank's take remains constant. The rest goes to you, the homeowner. By buying a home, you can seriously take advantage of the banks that are trying to take advantage of you. You may feel as though the interest and taxes are too high to really take advantage of homeownership, but the alternatives are even more costly.

Most people over the age of 60 will say that the best investment they ever made was buying their home. Most likely, they have gained a couple hundred thousand dollars or more in equity just by doing something they had to do anyway—live somewhere. On the other hand, if they had rented, they would have spent all that time just filling the pockets of their friendly landlord.

To calculate the amount someone might spend over the course of 5 years renting (something which I strongly recommend that you do), we'll assume rent stays the same for a fictional renter, Bob. Bob pays a nationally high, but regionally low $1,450 for his one bedroom condo in San Diego. Over the course of five years, he will have given his landlord $87,000 to help him travel the world on his 90 foot yacht. Bob's a nice fictional character, but this is too nice. We can assume that Bob needs that money more than his landlord and he's not even a good fictional landlord—Bob's fictional plumbing is always on the fritz and, of course, his landlord is never there to fix it!

Bob thinks that he's being fiscally prudent because he is spending less per month than if he had a mortgage payment for a similar condo ($2,000 a month). In a way he's correct in his thinking. When you factor in taxes, homeowners association fees, and maintenance costs, Bob is paying less per month by renting. However, none of the money he's paying is going into equity—he's throwing it all away.

With a home mortgage, the owner is, more often than not, putting a considerable amount toward the equity of the house each month. While a large chunk *is* going to the bank in the form of interest payment, that chunk is usually not as high as a rent payment. If we took into account all of the payments and costs of buying and maintaining a home, after 5 years, Bob would save $9,000 in payments by buying instead of renting. And, with the initial 10% down payment, he would have a total of $75,000 in equity (that's with a modest 2% increase in home price). Had he bought the condo, Bob would have almost as much in equity five years later as he would have paid in rent otherwise!

Bob would still earn money even if he didn't have the initial down payment of $30,000, though it would be considerably less due to the higher interest rate and higher percentage payment. Even if you look at your house as a liability rather than an asset, you should consider buying a house instead of renting.

18. Buy without an agent

While you're out there looking for your dream home, there are a couple of factors to keep in mind besides the typical factors of location, price, and condition. One aspect is the real estate agent (or lack thereof). While real estate agents can be helpful to you in your home search and assist with your questions about the process, they aren't necessary to buy or sell a house, and they can work against you in some respects, as we shall see later.

I'm no expert on the housing market, and I'm not an accountant or real estate mogul, but with the help of some close relatives, I purchased my home a couple years ago sans agent. Admittedly, we were very lucky with regard to finding the property—my brother and I were already living in it!

After two years of renting a place in San Diego, it became obvious that we were not being wise with our money by just giving it to our landlord. We were paying $1,850 per month, which turned out to be over $44,000 for the previous two years. In the mean time, the value of the townhouse we were living in had increased over $150,000 in value. Ultimately, we realized we had thrown away $44,000 and missed out on $150,000. So we decided to start looking for a place to buy.

A few weeks later, after lazily skimming the paper and Realtor.com, our landlord phoned us and said he was going to sell the unit and that we had to move out. What a surprise that was to us! Our landlord explained that he had a friend who wanted to buy our place for $385,000, which was well under the comparable sale prices in the area.

It turns out that the friend was living in Las Vegas, where new three-bedroom houses were going for less than *half* the $385,000 he was asking for our place. He wasn't quite sure what a two-bedroom townhouse was worth near the California coast. We asked if we could make the same offer or go even higher.

Unwilling to get into a bidding war in a distant land, the Vegas buyer backed out of his offer. Our then-landlord reassessed the value of the property and soon came to the realization that he could get about 10% more for it than what he was asking.

What followed was about two months of haggling and back-and-forth bargaining accompanied with the disappointment of rejected offers, shock of changed offers, and agony of dealing with an unsure seller. It was not a pleasant two months, to say the least.

They say that the three most stressful times in a persons life are getting married, losing a loved one, and buying a house, and I can attest to the latter as legitimately deserving to be on that list.

Buying a home can be an extremely stressful investment, and that is when you have a broker helping you. It's even more stressful if you want to buy the place directly from the owner without a broker. Needless to say, it is not an activity that everyone is cut out for, but doing so can be very lucrative, as explained above. A few weeks after we closed on our townhouse, an identical unit next door to ours sold for 10% above what we had paid.

Some of the lower sale price can be considered a discount for doing all the work that the brokers would have done. Brokers, after all, take, on average, 6% of the sale price to compensate for their hard work.

If brokers weren't in the equation, you and the seller could split the 6% that otherwise would have gone to them. We were fortunate enough to take full advantage of the 6% and then some with our purchase, though I wouldn't call it easy money. It's a difficult task to buy a house without a broker.

In our case, the seller benefited as well. He got roughly the same amount of money that he would have gotten at the market rate minus brokerage fees (the fees come out of the sale price—they aren't tacked on top of the sales price). With our specific situation, the seller was able to get away with doing far less work than normal sellers do. Since we had lived at the location for the previous two years, we were confident that the house wasn't about to fall down, and none of the usually seller-paid inspections were required.

The seller also didn't have to come out to the property and refurbish a somewhat rundown townhouse, by replacing the 15-year-old flooring and appliances. Since we were already living in the place, we knew exactly what we were getting and the seller was unsure what the place would look like to a third party. The seller was taking advantage of an easy sell with us.

This situation applies to most renter-landlord arrangements when the landlord looks to sell. While some residential property owners are looking to keep their properties for a long time, many would be willing to sell now if they knew their tenants were interested, especially in this "buyers' market". If you have been renting for a number of years and are happy with the place, look around for comparable prices and consider asking your landlord if he wants to sell.

At the time of this writing, it is a distinct open market for buyers and it doesn't look like this will be letting up any time soon. Your landlord has already made a considerable amount of money on the property in increased value and rental payments and may be willing to consider cashing in. It doesn't hurt to ask!

If you aren't ready to buy yet, ask if the landlord would be willing to consider a rent-to-own contract. With this situation, you pay your normal rent (sometimes it will be a little higher) for the specified period of time and if, at the end of your lease, you decide to buy, the rent that you have paid previously will be applied to the purchase price of the house. Landlords may be interested in this because they usually require a longer lease, and since there's a chance that the tenant may not end up purchasing the place, it's a win/win situation for them. If you decide to buy after the lease, the seller still gets all the benefits of selling to a tenant, as described above.

19. Decipher keywords on real estate listings

Good marketing has a way of making the ordinary or bad sound great. In the '70s, you may remember Ricardo Montalban turning the standard Chrysler Cordoba into a priceless luxury car. Who can resist the, "rich Corinthian Leather?" If you were wondering what Corinthian leather was when you first heard that, you weren't alone — the phrase was invented by marketers to make something ordinary (artificial leather, evidently) sound exotic and luxurious. It worked, if only for a while, before becoming the butt of many jokes.

The real estate industry has its world of marketing and tricks too. The words that agents use in describing their properties are always positive, yet sometimes they are factual and some are simply euphemistic. There is an entire code system that agents use to subtly feed information to buyers as well as make the property sound like a wonderful place to the person they are selling for. If you're buying a place, you should look out for words in the listing that don't really describe the property in straightforward terms.

Words like 'fantastic' or 'beautiful' really don't say anything specific—they're subjective and could mean different things to different people. Though they could inject a nice picture in your head, they shouldn't have any effect on your decision. In fact, a study by real estate agents has been conducted to determine what terms are associated with higher or lower sale prices. What they found was a number of words that are strongly linked to a lower sale price. In essence, certain words may sound good, but are empty and should be seen that way when you're looking through classified ads.

The words that are linked to lower prices are 'fantastic', 'spacious', 'charming', 'great neighborhood'. And there are usually exclamation marks at the end of each sentence! These phrases lack substance and even imply negative things. 'Great neighborhood', for instance, implies that this house may not be that great, but there are a lot of nice houses down the street.

Terms that have a positive link to price are 'granite', 'Corian', 'state of the art', 'maple', and 'gourmet'. While two of these terms ('state of the art' and 'gourmet') are ambiguous and subjective, they imply a higher echelon of taste, and thus money. The other words are specific descriptions of the physical characteristics of the house. Take advantage of these code words by differentiating the positive and negative ones.

'Well-maintained' is a great-sounding term, but it usually means that the place is old. It could be rephrased as 'the lime-green refrigerator and the orange laminate tile from the fifties are clean.' 'Pristine', 'well-kept', 'immaculate', and 'mint' are similar terms with similar meanings.

'Brand new' is a house that is one to five years old, but is pre-owned, whereas 'new-construction' means that you'll be the first owner. 'Move-in condition' means that people can close and move in on the same day, without any repairs or replacements.

'Must-see' implies that it may be in an ugly neighborhood, but it's nice inside. If you're looking at a 'quaint' house, it'll probably be old and small. 'Charming' or 'cozy' are newer, but they're still small. 'Needs TLC' probably means the roof is about to fall down, and 'luxury' means there are probably a few gold-plated things placed in conspicuous locations. 'Convenient' means that the house is located under a freeway overpass, while 'urban setting' means that you'll be used to the sounds of the local bar in a matter of weeks.

With regard to the pricing of the house, a 'motivated seller' doesn't mean that the owner is a go-getter; it means that the price is negotiable and the seller wants to get rid of the property soon. 'Won't last' means that they priced the house well under the market value to sell it quickly. It could also mean that the house is a unique one or in a desirable neighborhood.

20. Make the real estate agents work for you

If you are on the other side of the equation and you are trying to sell your house, there are a couple things you should keep in mind regarding your real estate agent. The first thing that you should know is that, naturally, real estate agents usually sell their own homes. When they do, though, they keep them on the market for an average of three weeks longer than when they are selling for other people.

By keeping their homes on the market an average of three weeks longer, realtors end up selling their homes for an average of 3% more. When you have an agent selling for you, make him or her work for you by showing the house until you get your price.

An agent's main goal is to sell the house, period. If the house they're selling goes for around $300,000, they'll make just about $9,000, which is half of the 6% broker commission. Half of that money usually goes to their branch office, leaving them with $4,500. If they can sell the house for $290,000, they're still making about the same ($4,350), but the owner misses out on almost ten grand. To you this is a big deal, but to the broker, it's a minor detail. If you're already paying such a large chunk of change to sell your house, get your money's worth by leaving the house on the market until a buyer who wants to pay your price comes along.

21. Let someone else help you build a real estate empire

I can't speak about this technique personally because I haven't purchased any investment properties yet, but the idea has been promoted thoroughly and should be included here. If you have equity that you would like to earn money on, an investment home is a great way to do just that. Buy a house and let the renters pay for your mortgage. If you have a substantial down payment (about 30%), the mortgage rates are good enough still that you can cover your entire mortgage cost with the rent payment that you would collect from your tenants in most markets.

If you're interested in a second home and have the time to attract and organize the tenants, a property in a tourist area might be the ticket. A friend of mine recently bought a vacation home on the East Coast. Weekly rental prices during the peak season nearly cover the mortgage for the entire year, and he gets to enjoy a few weeks of the year at the house, making the deal even sweeter.

Franklin Says:
"He that would Fish, must venture his bait. "

The Culprit: car dealers and real estate agents

The Target: pride, location, information disadvantage

Ad-In requires: patience, some real estate know-how

What Ben Earned/Saved:
• value of owned car (after 5 years)	$7,000
• savings for buying 1-year pre-owned car	$4,200
• buy the new car in the country	$250
• 1-year equity earned by owning house	$15,000
• buying home without agent	$12,000
• keeping house on market 3 more weeks	$9,700
Total	$48,150

Part Five

The Marketing Game

"Advertising may be described as the science of arresting the human intelligence long enough to get money from it."

-Stephen Leacock

"Many a small thing has been made large by the right kind of advertising."

-Mark Twain

Hi there! I just wanted to take a moment to thank you, the readers of this book, for being so wise in your selection. You must be interested in saving and making money and getting the most out of your everyday financial transactions—you and I have that in common. You must be one of the wise ones—one that will inevitably become wealthy and happy. Thanks, and congratulations. We've come to an integral section in the book in which we're going to discuss, not big purchases and institutions in this economy, but all of the smaller companies and retailers patronized by everyone. I know you are interested in how these companies are trying to take advantage of us consumers because you bought this book, so this section should be a pleasure. Plus, it's full of scientific studies that are backed by some of the greatest minds in the consumer science fields. It's only one small chapter, but it's very valuable, so enjoy it.

That was my best attempt at a sales pitch for this chapter based on the same psychological techniques that marketers have been using for the last century to help take advantage of our natural urges.

Throughout the 20th century, as marketing and advertising have become an ever-growing facet of the business world and our lives in general, techniques in influencing behavior or mentality have become a science. Psychologists and marketers alike have employed countless studies in order to understand intrinsic human urges, all with the ultimate aim of persuading you, the consumer, to do something they want. The result has been a century of propaganda, from wartime cant in the political arena to consumer spending. Whether you like it or not, you have most likely been the unwitting target of many of these techniques.

Have you ever wondered what compelled you to buy a specific item that you saw on television but didn't really need? Ever wondered why you donated to one charity, when there are so many other good ones out there? Have you ever wondered why you have desperately "needed" certain gadgets only to use them a few times before forgetting about them? Has it ever struck you as odd that you'll search through coupon books for hours a week to save 40 cents on a box of cereal, but you won't bat an eye at the $99 finance charge tacked on to your credit card debt each month? These circumstances may be rooted in the very nature of human sociality. Companies, politicians, and even friends and family in some way may all be using persuasive techniques in order to get you to do something or buy something.

In all cases, these companies, politicians, and friends are trying to take advantage of you. It doesn't seem like they are — in fact it seems like *you* are the one making the decisions. After all, it is a free country and you are the one deciding whether or not to buy the Chelsea sofa or the English sofa at Crate & Barrel, but if you knew what techniques were being used to lead you to those decisions, you may not have acted the same way. Just as the tendency for Americans to spend beyond their means is seemingly ingrained into our culture, there are a number of tendencies ingrained in us as humans, which promote others' ability to take advantage of us and sometimes act against our best interests.

Robert B. Cialdini, famed psychologist at Arizona State University, has noted that there are five of tendencies in humans that can be taken advantage of: reciprocation, social validation, liking, authority, and scarcity. Those familiar with supply and demand may notice the last one on the list as an obvious clue to infer the value of something. If there are only two hundred widgets in the world, no matter what they do, they can be considered pretty valuable. The use of scarcity in sales can be seen on TV ads that urge the buyer to buy soon because, "This offer is good for a limited time only!" A human's innate urge is to jump on that deal simply because of the scarcity. This example illustrates how integral our urges can be and how powerful they can be when used to take advantage of others.

The goal in this book is not to encourage the use of these techniques to make others do things for you. However, the knowledge of human psychology with respect to others trying to take advantage of you may help you avoid being taken advantage of. In turn, you will be able to get the most out of those companies and people when you're aware of all the factors involved.

Most everyone is trying to influence your decisions though not all for greedy, disagreeable purposes. It's possible that you've received a donation request from the charity organization, Disabled American Veterans, as I have. It seems like a good organization, helping people who have devoted part or most of their lives to defend their country. It is a worthy cause, but, on the other hand, there are so many worthy causes, the reality is that one person can't give to all of them. The DAV charity has a differential advantage, though, and it's that they actually give *to* the people from whom they are asking donations. Reciprocation, Cialdini's first tendency, is an urge that comes into play in this situation. After I received a package from the organization including a gift (free mailing labels) I was grateful. Consciously unaware of the reciprocation tendency, I mentioned to a friend of mine that I might donate to DAV because, after all, they gave me those nice address labels.

The urge to reciprocate works in other situations too, most notably in concessions. When you hear an announcer bring down the price at the end of a commercial, this is a concession, and it usually compels the buyer to return the favor and make the purchase.

"This handy thingamajig sells for over $300 in the store, but we're giving you a serious discount because you're watching television at 3 a.m.; you can get it for just $49.99!" an announcer may proclaim. Isn't it telling that most of these *concessions* start with a large round number (like $100), but end up a small figure with a lot of nines? Many of us may see right past this veiled attempt at convincing us of a discount, but if the original price seems reasonable, the discounted price may well put the consumer over the top with the urge to concede.

Consistency is another urge that we humans have, an urge that companies may use to their benefit. We want to remain consistent with our actions so as to be true to ourselves, and this means that we will maintain our opinions despite mounting evidence against them, and we will even buy something we don't need in order to comply with previous statements. Politicians get people on their side by sponsoring petitions for certain causes. When someone signs their name to an issue affiliated with a candidate, they're much more likely to vote for that candidate at a later time. "You support better education; vote for candidate A!"

Advertising image is a way to encourage the consistency tendency too. When you see an ad for Coke containing people you can identify with, you're more likely to choose Coke when faced with the decision at the supermarket. When you identify with an ad, you are making it difficult for yourself to be inconsistent and buy a competitor's product later just because it was less expensive.

In this way, consistency is related to two other persuasive techniques: liking and authority. It makes a lot of sense that you're more willing to say yes to someone you like as opposed to someone you have a bad opinion of. Also, an authority figure is more likely to convince people to do something. Cialdini reported that even minor indicators of authority were enough to encourage people to do something. University of Texas researchers Lefkowitz, Blake, and Mouton found in 1955 that 350% more people followed a person walking across the street on a do-not-walk light when he was wearing a suit and tie as opposed to casual attire. This shows that people tend to put more trust in those they think are figures of authority, even if what they're doing is unusual or generally considered wrong.

Another human tendency, social validation, may be the strongest desire that humans have nowadays regarding their reasons for making purchases. If you don't think so, just marvel at the price a white T-shirt can fetch when a trendy name is screen-printed on the front. Social validation, which can also be termed *coolness*, is so strong it practically drives the market these days. No longer do we obey our innate desires to eat, sleep, and protect our lives and property; we instead obey our desire to encourage other people to like us. Just like the desires that our culture has bypassed, our culture has helped diminish any idea of true value that a consumer may have. Though a $2 T-shirt covers one's skin the same way a $50 Bebe T-shirt does, the coolness of the more expensive shirt makes it sell.

The PBS documentary *Scientific American Frontiers* explored the idea of coolness in people and reported that the brain actually becomes intensely active when certain cool and uncool things are presented. They reported that there are two types of people: those whose brains light up or are stimulated when they see things that are cool, and those whose brains light up when they see things that are *un*cool. Either way, humans usually have strong reactions to the coolness of a retail item and the probability that will be validated socially. This coolness factor makes a big difference in the way consumers make purchases, and marketers are eager to exploit this urge.

There are at least two variations of the social validation urge with regard to consumer purchases: 1) an urge to buy things that everyone has or is talking about, and 2) an urge to be ahead of the pack or the first one to do something and to be original and unique. While the first urge promotes follower status and is almost a sure bet with marketers, it may not be the most effective goal. A more effective marketing technique is to attempt to gain the early adopters, who set the trends for the mass population. While the followers can catch on to a trend and make money, the companies that are the first of their kind are the ones that make a major impact financially. Of course, the latter goal is more risky and not as easily attainable.

Though the early adopters set the trends that people will follow a long time down the line, trends don't always catch on, and the process of starting a trend is extremely difficult, especially in the retail market. One of the keys to starting trends is social validation.

To demonstrate the process of starting a trend through social validation, a number of City University of New York professors (Milgram, Bickman, and Berkowitz) conducted an experiment in the 1960s. In the experiment, a man stopped on a crowded sidewalk in the city and looked up to the sky at nothing in particular for 60 seconds. This behavior caused very few of the surrounding passers–by to take notice or change their own behavior. However, when four more people were added to the experiment and all were instructed to stop and look upward, the reaction of the bystanders changed. When only one person was looking up at nothing, only 4 percent joined him. When five people were doing the same thing, the amount of people who joined them increased to 18%. When fifteen people were looking up at nothing, 40% of the passers by joined them.

Peer pressure has a dramatic effect on people, and since the effect is not always obvious, we generally go along with it. In other words, we're being taken advantage of, and we don't even seem to mind.

We want to drive the expensive car that everyone agrees is luxurious and high-class; we want to wear the designer clothes that everyone wishes they could afford; and we (at least the female of the species) want the top of the line cosmetics. Amazingly, though, this desire to have what everyone wants forces us to pay for things that are worth a small fraction of what we actually buy them for. With respect to the cosmetics reference, John Stossel, in his book *Give Me a Break*, describes an investigative report he did on these make-up *mark-ups*.

In the story, Stossel had discovered that high-end cosmetics companies Adrian Arpel, Diane von Furstenberg, Calvin Klein, and Stagelight were all selling the same eye shadow that a generic company sold for dramatically less. Stossel's producer got an offer to buy the product for $1 per half-ounce, and the companies mentioned above were selling the same amount of the same substance for $33, $35, $45, and $50, respectively. This demonstrates how powerful a name can be in the social validation game. People are willing to spend perhaps 1,000% of the true value of an item just because they think it is socially esteemed. In Stossel's report, the Stagelight president was quoted as saying that the generic brand and his brand may come from the same place, "but, our customers don't *believe* that."

So, what do all those tendencies have to do with personal finance, you might ask. If you haven't already caught on to some of these techniques as they are used in the real world, you should make a concerted effort to do so.

By understanding these tendencies (reciprocation, social validation, liking, authority, and scarcity), which marketers are trying to elicit, you will have an upper hand when you are making your purchases, even when it comes to retail goods. You will be able to identify which products are perhaps overpriced or which items you really have no need for but feel strangely compelled to buy. In addition, you could use these tendencies in your favor by invoking the same urges in the person who's selling you something and get better service, better deals, and an overall better purchasing experience.

22. Assess the value of your favorite brand

As a result of a number of the tendencies mentioned above, namely consistency, liking, and social validation, people become attached to certain brands. They overlook true value and fulfill their natural urges by spending more money on items they've always bought, or whose salespeople are nice, or which brand names evoke the idea of coolness among others. These are natural, understandable tendencies, but they are important to acknowledge when you are trying to avoid being taken advantage of. There are options other than your favorite brand that match the quality or even surpass it in terms of price. Once you can defeat the natural tendencies that urge you to throw money away, you will open the door to a vast array of options.

Currently, major players in retailing are the generic brands that offer products similar to the name-brand goods at significant discounts. This can be seen most dramatically in foodstuffs, where Great Value (one of Wal-Mart's leading brands), for example, has gained significant market share in recent years. Private labels like Great Value produce goods for a specific retailer and make up 25% of the retail market in the U.S. and 45% of the European market.

You may be sentimentally stuck on your favorite brand and can't imagine buying some generic food item, but is your loyalty rewarded? By sticking with a brand regardless of its price, you could be wasting money. Often, quality is not jeopardized with the reduction of price, and you are just purchasing a prettier package design or simple logo recognition for 200% of the cost of a generic brand. Other times the quality is seriously compromised as in a staple food of mine, whole grain wheat crackers. Albertson's Woven Wheat Crackers taste worse than the name brand Triscuits, and they include less expensive and less healthy trans fats like partially hydrogenated oils. In cases like these, it is certainly recommended that you stick with the name brand to maintain a standard in quality. However, most generic brands are equal in quality to their more expensive counterparts.

While name brands take advantage of the consumer by playing on consistency and social validation, generic brands take advantage of you as a customer too. It's easy for retailers to sell their own items at their store because they already have a customer base. It's up to you as a consumer to take advantage of their discounted price and maintain quality.

Generics are gaining in popularity, and, with that popularity, quality is also increasing. In industries besides the food industry, the quality is basically equivalent to that of the name brand. A plastic and rubber toothbrush is just as effective if it doesn't say Oral-B or Mentadent on the handle. Similarly, when a production formula or snazzy design patent is released by a name brand, the generic market is bound to come up with a high-quality and low-price alternative.

After I purchased my iMac, I looked into buying additional RAM (sorry about the geek talk here—RAM is a type of memory that every computer has; more is better). Apple was offering 1 GigaByte of RAM for $300, but the generic version selling at another store was $110. There is nothing that compares to Apple's computer design or performance, but the company's prices for add-ons do not match market prices.

Another industry in which generics are becoming more popular and more controversial at the same time is the pharmaceutical industry. In a recent report by the federal government, one of the only bright spots in the overall price of healthcare in this country was the average cost for prescription drugs. The major influx of generics has led to a decrease in the price consumers pay per prescription. In addition, more generic versions are on their way to the market. The number of applications for generic drug approvals by the U.S. Food and Drug Administration has nearly tripled in recent years, foretelling an increase in the competition with expensive brand-name drugs. This is all good news for consumers of prescription drugs, but they have to take advantage of these options, not avoid them because of sophisticated marketing techniques by the name brands.

While the lower average price per prescription is good for us the consumers, it's not good for the multi-million dollar pharmaceutical companies that stand to lose half of their market share to generic drugs. They will do everything they can to prevent competition for their products, including lobbying Congress to prevent citizens from seeking out prescriptions in Canada and lobbying the government to slow down its approval of generics. During the 250% increase of applications to the FDA per year since 2001, the Office of Generic Drugs, the office that handles the applications (and could probably use some creative marketing itself considering its bland name), has remained relatively constant with regard to number of employees. There's more work, but a static workforce. So, it's evident that third parties will be putting up a lot of resistance to the increase in generic brand sales, but that shouldn't deter you from taking advantage of these products.

If you insist on keeping with the name brand, another option you have in order to take advantage of a company's pricing is to choose a different variety or flavor. Established brands usually offer significant discounts when they come out with a new line or flavor. Thus, you may be able to find your favorite snack or drink in a new variety for a significant discount. 30% may not sound like a big deal on $1.20, but if you make purchases like that often, it can really add up.

Also, look for comparable products that may have better

deals associated with them. Most of America enjoys a glass of orange juice at breakfast. They might say that orange juice is a perfect flavor complement to cold cereal or sausage and eggs, and it provides 100% Recommended Daily Allowance of vitamin C. If the last reason is the most important to you, though, you may be interested to find that apple juice made with all-natural juice usually has 100% RDA or more of vitamin C added as well.

Simply because orange juice has been marketed as *the* breakfast drink that everyone must have, it is generally more expensive than other drinks that are just as healthy and just as appropriate for breakfast. If you consider all fruit juices for your morning beverage, you open up competition for orange juice that should provide you a less expensive drink. Sure, I like orange juice, but is it worth $1 more for a half-gallon?

23. Be nice to the customer service representatives

While what you buy is the most important factor in your purchase experience, from whom you buy it is also important. Whether you're buying kitchen appliances at The Home Depot or antiques at a garage sale, you can stand to benefit from your brief relationship with the seller. Just as you wouldn't care to buy something from someone you didn't like, the reverse is true; someone isn't going to go out of his way to give you a deal if he doesn't like you. One shouldn't just be nice to get something in return, but sometimes when dealing with a salesperson, you have to be just as much of a salesperson to get what you deserve. In purchasing situations, you can use liking, reciprocation, consistency, and scarcity effectively for your cause.

Liking: let the salesperson know that you've done retail before, or ask how sales are going today. Ask if they get commission, and let them know that you want to help them out. And, as always, a smile goes a very long way. We've all experienced the unruly customer who is yelling and abrasive and demeaning toward the employees at a retail store. That person will most likely get what he or she wants, but the employees aren't going to give any more than that. It goes without saying, but I'm going to say it anyway, if someone wants helpful, courteous service, it helps to be friendly too.

Reciprocation: inform the salesperson that you've made a serious effort to get to their store or residence. You can also start with offering a small purchase, then adding to it if they give you a better deal.

Consistency: when you initiate communication with the seller, ask about an ad you saw stating that their store professed to have the best prices around and whether or not that was true. Once they've committed to that idea, mention the sale you saw in the newspaper that day at another store and ask if they can match the lower price. Even if it's not the policy of the store to offer such a deal, they've already professed that their price would be cheaper, and they will work hard to ensure that.

Scarcity: let sales people know that you could be using your money for other things and that you don't have money to throw away. This should be evident, but if the salesperson can better appreciate your financial situation, he they may do more to get your sale.

These techniques are used on you to get you to buy things — why not use them on the people who are using them on you?

24. Be patient with big purchases

Last year my family and I remodeled our house with new flooring and paint along with some other minor fixes. We did some research on carpet and flooring and went with The Home Depot for most of our purchases. The deal that we were going to take advantage of was a $200 gift certificate on every purchase of $2,000 or more. What we weren't aware of was that that particular offer was available pretty much every week. A week after we made the purchase for the carpet, we received another offer in the mail for 10% off the entire purchase of flooring (a substantial increase in savings).

The Home Depot customer service was extremely helpful and gave us the discount on our purchase even though we had purchased it before the promotional period has started. They were nice in that respect, but most stores and most customer service personnel are not so accommodating. The moral we learned was to be patient about purchases of this nature because there may just be a better deal right around the corner.

If you're in the market for electronics or computer equipment, patience can have multiple effects on your purchase, positive and negative. WARNING: the next few sentences may contain extremely boring technical jargon! In 2002, when I purchased my iMac by Apple, I was anxious to buy the sleek, high-quality computer. I did my research and knew that it was a solid computer.

I decided to purchase the 800 GHz iMac with a 15" screen and first attempted to buy the computer at Comp USA for $5 less than at an Apple Store. It was an excruciating experience, and I don't recommend shopping at Comp USA to anyone. I applied for their credit card to receive an additional discount and was rejected due to a security check I had placed at the credit check company to prevent fraud. Then, I attempted to use a family member's card to utilize the frequent flyer miles benefit and, though they were speaking with this family member, they couldn't proceed with the purchase. I then couldn't use my own credit card because I didn't have ID (my fault). I was furious after spending so much time on this and having nothing to show for it.

I should have taken the hint—maybe I wasn't supposed to buy the computer then. After the Comp USA debacle, I purchased my computer at the Apple Store, and I was thrilled with the product and very happy with the purchase process. A few months later, however, Apple introduced an upgraded iMac with a gigabyte processor (25% better than the one I had) and a 17" screen (a lot better than mine) for less money than what I spent on mine! I was a little distraught, to say the least. If that happened today, I probably would have tried to make an exchange for the updated computer, but I didn't at the time and kept the original.

I was happy with my purchase, and I hadn't foreseen such a drastically better deal a matter of weeks after my purchase. Don't let my mistake happen to you. When it comes to computers, you can usually expect a better product for less at some point in the near future. Some other electronics, like televisions for some reason, don't follow this trend, and prices for them just continue to go up without the option of a dramatically better product. When a computer is a few months old, you can almost always count on a better one coming onto the market and selling for less.

However, if you keep waiting until they come out with the computer to end all computers, you may be waiting for a few thousand years. The idea is to wait until the next great computer comes out. This way, you will know that you are getting at least a few months of top-of-the-line equipment.

Though this doesn't apply to all retail goods, patience is still a valuable virtue with most purchases. There are a number of factors you can use to your benefit if you're planning on making a big purchase.

The time of year can have an impact on the tactics retail stores are willing to use to entice you into shopping at their place. There are always the after-Christmas discounts that bring in more people year after year, and generally speaking, cheaper clothing can be found off-season. These are obvious times to wait for when considering substantial purchases.

If you're looking for a more general trend, you can look at the Consumer Price Index (CPI), or what inflation is based on. The CPI data seem to indicate that a few months are particularly cheaper than others. From 2002 to 2005, consumer prices regularly *decreased* in month over month percentage change in the April-May-June quarter. This indicates that stores may be willing to offer larger discounts on big purchases during these months. This was proven when we made the carpet purchase mentioned above. We initially purchase our carpet in March, only to learn of a better discount soon after in April, which supports our CPI finding.

The data showed that other months are particularly bad for the Consumer Price Index. January is generally associated with a higher CPI, contrary to what one may think during the post-holiday sales blitzkrieg. This was also the case with February. Even when excluding highly volatile industries like food and energy, those months usually see high increases in CPI.

If you are determined to make a purchase at a particular store, ask the employees whether there will be sales on the item you're purchasing in the near future. Also, if you have a favorite store, they may have a newsletter or mailing list to alert you to upcoming sales and bargains.

A friend of mine has another technique she uses to get the best deal on something. When she can wait to purchase something she likes, she places it on layaway and then buys it when it goes on sale or when there's another incentive on the item. I'd never heard of layaway, much less used it, but my friend says it works like a charm.

25. Only use coupons when you need the item

The marketing-savvy salesman in the play I referenced in this book's introduction who was able to sell a slightly damaged suit for the original price because it was "marked down" illustrates one thing very clearly: A discount isn't always a discount. This is especially true when the purchaser is interested in just the bargain and not really interested in the actual item. A $10 discount on a shirt that you'll never wear means that you've wasted $30, not that you've saved $10. It's common sense that, in order to take advantage of those who are trying to take advantage of you, you should only buy discounted items for which you have a genuine need. In other words, acknowledge that the seller is trying to evoke reciprocation and reject it.

A good technique to help you understand whether you really want the item is to sleep on it. You can avoid impulse buys by returning to the deal the next day and reassessing your desire for the item. The salesman will tell you that the deal won't last or that the product will sell out if you wait — so let it. There will always be other deals, and, if it truly is a good deal, the salesman doesn't need to be pushy. Sleep on it and come back to it the next day. If the item is still appealing and still available, buy it, but don't use it. Consider it for a few days and return it if you decide you'd rather spend your money in a better way.

26. Shop the competition

When you're in the market for a purchase above $50, try your favorite store, but also shop the competition. While doing so, make it clear to the salespeople that you know of other deals and bargains at other stores. It's likely that many stores will match the low prices of another store or go out of their way to make you happy in order to gain your business.

In our remodeling process last year, we decided to go with The Home Depot for all of our flooring because we appreciated their customer service, and it seemed simple to use just one vendor. The Home Depot farms out its flooring jobs, though, and we weren't so happy with the affiliate assigned to us for our kitchen tile installment. The company's employees were not very good at either customer service or creativity and couldn't even complete the job. When we spoke to another flooring specialist in the area and told him our situation, he was ecstatic to potentially draw customers from The Home Depot, so he gave us a nice discount. In that case, we were able to utilize The Home Depot's easy-to-access flooring displays and helpful customer service and get the actual product from another source for less.

With the Internet, shopping the competition has become a science. There are entire sites dedicated to finding the best price for a particular item. Google's Froogle (a clever take on 'frugal') takes your search string and returns thousands of items that fit your query, which can be sorted by price, category, and vendor. Stores are listed on the site complete with consumer rating and all the other products they sell.

You may want to actually see the product you're spending thousands of dollars on and not trust a one-paragraph description online. In that case, you can go to a physical store like Best Buy and get your hands on the product to analyze and scrutinize it, then look it up on Froogle to ensure you're paying the least expensive price. Take advantage of certain retailers' consumer interaction displays and others' great prices. It may take a little more time, but it could be worth 20% of the purchase price or more.

Another case where you should definitely shop the competition is auto mechanics. Sure, the process of finding just one auto mechanic can be daunting, not to mention multiple mechanics, but if you want to avoid being ripped off, a second opinion on your check-engine light may be in order. Mechanics usually charge a fee just to look at a car but will sometimes deduct the diagnosis charge from the ultimate repair cost. This process deters the type of second-opinion shopping that benefits consumers, thus enabling a few habits for mechanics: price gauging and mysterious charges. When a car is acting up or worse, is inoperable, the owner most likely just wants to get it fixed and back on the road. He doesn't want to wait day after day and deal with multiple mechanics to ensure that he isn't being taken advantage of. But this impetuousness is just what many mechanics rely on to overcharge their customers.

Auto mechanics have what is called an information advantage, which means, simply, that they know much more about your car than you would ever want to know. The greater their information advantage, the greater their ability to rip you off. Just by going to two different auto shops, you reduce their information advantage and can deal with the problem that much more effectively. To be sure, there are good, moral mechanics out there, but you will never know that yours is good until you shop the competition, and more specifically, shop the competition in regard to a particular problem.

While you're doing this, avoid telling the mechanics that you are getting a second opinion. The less they know, the more you are maintaining your information advantage. If two mechanics come up with the exact same diagnosis for your car's problem, you know that they are probably being on the level with you. If one of your mechanics tacks on a couple extra repairs to the one repair the other shop recommended, the one repair should suffice. Though a mechanic's information advantage is high, he doesn't know everything, and, as you'll read in the next part of this book, all mechanics may lack knowledge in specific auto repairs. It's best to shop around to get them working for you again.

27. Is 10% worth 10 minutes?

Almost every major retail outfit has its own credit card and they are willing to give you a hefty discount on purchased items if you sign up for one. When you walk into a Target or a Macy's, you are sure to find an employee sitting at a makeshift sign-up stand offering major discounts on your purchases that day if you sign up for their affinity credit card (a card that is supported by a third party financial institution).

As we explained earlier, extra cards aren't necessarily bad for your credit, and they can be good as long as you pay your debt off monthly. So, if there isn't an annual fee for the card, all you are losing if you sign up for the card is the 10 minutes it takes to fill out the application.

Of course, the need for an extra credit card isn't why you would apply—you would apply because you want the 10-20% they are willing to take off your shopping bill. Is ten minutes of your time worth the amount that you save? It depends. If your goal is to make a very large purchase, like an office set or a computer or a home entertainment center, the savings could be a few hundred dollars. In that case, it would be foolish *not* to sign up for the credit card. If you are just going in to buy a pair of socks, the credit card is probably not the best idea.

If you do sign up for the card, you may want to destroy the card after you make your purchase. If you don't want to add to your debt subconsciously, take it to the trash. To fully take advantage of this offer, sign up, shop, cut the card up, and pay it off immediately. It's possible that you could receive the 10% discount for a large purchase by signing up for the card, then canceling the card after paying it off and repeating the process the next year. Some companies would be weary if they see that type of behavior, but some accept it because they are really eager for credit card customers or because they're so big, they can't keep track of all their old customers. Either way, it doesn't hurt to try.

Something to keep in mind is that your decision to apply for the card and receive the discount shouldn't convince you to buy a bunch of things that you had no intention or desire to purchase before you walked into the store. Besides getting in on the highly profitable credit industry, the ploy of the retailer is to get you to buy more with their card than you otherwise would have. Don't let them take advantage of you like that! Be diligent in keeping to the items that you need.

In fact, it may be wise to look for what you need first and then find a store that is willing to give you a decent discount on a credit card to make that purchase. The offers are everywhere and can be found as easily as typing a few words on your Internet browser. The first two retailers I looked up online (Target and Office Depot) were both offering 20% off purchases that day for signing up for their affinity credit card. It's likely that whatever you need can be found at a store that is offering a similar deal.

The main issue with these offers is that they create obscure debt. If you do as I recommend and cut up the card after the first use, you may forget that you have an extra $759.22 in debt out there, especially if part of the deal is that you don't have to make a payment for the first 3 months after the purchase. People go on without budgeting in that extra purchase because it's not part of their normal financial routine. To help avoid the obscure debt, we recommend that you intentionally set aside the exact amount of money that you will need to pay the new card off when the time comes (often two months or more after the purchase).

28. You're spending a couple grand; the least they can offer you is a printer

Have you ever wondered why infomercials or TV-only deals usually end with, ". . . and wait, that's not all!" They are using a marketing technique to put you over the top in your desire to purchase their product. If a certain deal sounds pretty good for a product, you may consider it, but when there is an additional gift added to the deal at no extra cost, you'll be much more likely to make the purchase.

"If you think that is a good deal, just wait 'til you see what comes with it!" is a common sales pitch on most infomercials. When I looked up the most common seen-on-TV products online, I noticed quite a few had the free product along with the image of the product for sale. The idea is brilliant and very effective. Attempt to sell half of something for the full price, then include the full product, and voila, you have an irresistible bargain!

Oftentimes, salespeople will not bring up the over-the-top extra if you seem interested enough in the original deal. On a recent computer purchase, a customer service rep was helping me with an item. She was very informative and answered all of my questions. When I asked if there were any deals being offered, she said that they were offering a $100 rebate on a $100 printer. I seriously doubt she would have suggested that rebate if I hadn't asked her, but she was willing to provide that information because it could have helped convince me to make the purchase. I probably would have bought the computer anyway, but she didn't know that. Who knows what other offers she would have come up with to convince me to buy their product if I had held out. When making a big purchase like a computer, the least they can do is give you a printer.

29. Buy in bulk only when you need it

Just as there is a love of the bargain in the United States, there is also a strong inclination to waste, especially with regard to food. Rarely do we finish off our gigantic-sized meals when we dine out, and very few of us are scraping the bottom of the sauce containers. And who wants to eat the last grubby piece of crumpled-up bread in a loaf?

Marketers have known that these two tendencies (to get a bargain and to waste) are prevalent in this country and they work to exploit them. When people shop for food or look to order something on the menu, they're not looking solely at the price; they're looking at the price per pound. This type of shopping fits both of the American tendencies to look for bargains and consequently waste but is extremely unwise if you plan on taking advantage of the people who are trying to take advantage of you. Ten cents an ounce may sound good at the store, but when you throw away the last third of the product because you bought too much, the value is diminished.

30. Need a new cell phone?

Cell phone companies make up one of the most opportunistic of consumer industries when it comes to taking advantage of their customers. While cell phone usage is booming (over 200 million users in the U.S. alone) and resulting in double-digit profit growth for companies in the industry like Qualcomm, Motorola, and Texas Instruments, the corporations that actually deal with the consumers are finding ways to really profit off of them (that'd be you and me).

It starts with the ever-so-friendly and ubiquitous service contract that providers require for you to purchase their service. At first glance, a contract for such a service seems bizarre to me when I look at it objectively—I don't have to sign a contract with my internet or cable company; nor do I have to sign a two-year deal with any utility, like a water or electricity company. These companies (with the exception of internet service) are all basically monopolies based on my location and despite what you remember from your childhood playing the board game, monopolies are not fun and games. I'm not sure about you, but whenever I played Monopoly the board game, I usually ended up owning B&O Railroad and St. James Place and nothing else. I would usually dread the last row of properties where some lucky little jerk put up hotels on all the green properties and both Boardwalk and Park Place. That lucky little guy who got the monopoly on all the good streets is equivalent to many utility companies today.

Unfortunately, I can't get my home electricity from ten different companies, and I'm pretty much forced to patronize one. With mobile phone companies on the other hand, the consumer has many options and there is such a great startup cost in gaining new customers that they have to institute contracts to make it profitable for them. This is bad because contracts are tough to break, but good because it means these profitable phone companies can offer us deals to bring in our business.

Once the wireless companies have you in their grips with a long-term contract, they can pretty much dictate the company/customer relationship. In addition, the government loves to get in on the act as well—your first bill (as many readers have already noticed) will host a variety of extraneous charges, fees, and surcharges. Just as long-distance landline phone carriers have become synonymous with fees, so have their descendants, the cell phone companies. You may have signed up for a $59.99 a month service, but may not have expected to pay the Regulatory Program Charge ($1.75), the Federal Universal Service Fund Surcharge ($1.21), the State Public Utility Surcharge ($.50), the Federal Excise Tax ($1.34), the State E911 Tax ($.28) and more fees and charges, ad nauseam. Cell phone companies aren't directly responsible for most of these fees, but for some reason your base monthly cell phone price doesn't include these extra costs. My phone bill costs me an average of 25% more than the rate plan fee of $39.99 each month.

Other industries have similar price additions from taxes and charges but are scrutinized more because they're not listed individually as in a phone bill. A favorite topic of chronic complainers nowadays is the evil gasoline companies, which are bringing in profits that make Bill Gates' and the Sultan of Brunei's mouths water. The gas companies are getting beat up over their wealth because, even though a large chunk of the price of gas is the result of government taxes and fees (about 20% throughout the country), we don't see those fees. When we go to fill up, we think we're giving all $3.29 a gallon to the doughnut-chomping executives in Exxon Mobile, not to the government too. Cell phone companies are smart and make it clear that not all of what you pay goes to the doughnut-chomping executives of Cingular. The fees on your cell phone bill are designated for a number of different things, very few of which are doughnuts for the company's executives.

In California, when you buy a wireless service, you're not only paying for your service, you're also paying for telephone service in low-income housing (the Universal Lifeline fee- $.57), and libraries and schools (the Teleconnect fee- $.05). According to the California government, we also pay to, "keep basic telephone service affordable in high cost areas," with the California High Cost Fund B ($.87). There's also a California High Cost Fund A for basically the same purpose. In a not-so-unusual flash of myopia, the government has forced a new technology to subsidize a dying technology—cell phone customers are paying to reduce the price of traditional telephone service! So, not only is your cell phone service provider taking advantage of you when you purchase a cell phone, so is your friendly neighborhood government.

Your contract probably explains most of this, though cell phone companies can change the contract at any time without notifying you.

But wait, that's not all! There's more fun with cell phone bills! If you want to switch service plans, you will usually incur a substantial fee. If you want to cancel your service, you're looking at an enormous fee ($200 or more with some carriers). With contracts like the ones cell phone companies use, it's easy for them to take advantage of their consumers. Additionally, most mobile phone companies treat their current customers worse and offer them inferior deals than non-customers. If you are thinking about signing a contract with a mobile company or have a contract about to expire, you can begin to take advantage of these companies that are clearly taking advantage of you.

Most brands, like Cingular or T-Mobile, offer free phones with your contract, sometimes giving you a $200 phone for free after a discount and mail-in rebate. As usual, on-line purchases give you additional savings.

If your current contract is up soon, you have more bargaining power than you probably expect. You can usually get a nicer phone than you currently have with upgraded service terms (more minutes per month) for less when you switch carriers. Most consumers are hesitant to switch carriers because they want to keep the same phone number. Luckily, that's not an issue with new portability laws that allow you to keep your number when you switch providers, even when you switch from a landline to a cell-phone service.

Unfortunately, you do not have the bargaining power while you are an obediently loyal paying customer — to get the edge on these gigantic communications companies, you must drop their service. When your contract is up, it's almost too easy to get the offer that you want and deserve.

My first phone service extravaganza reveals the silliness of the situation and the ability that we have to take advantage of these uncommon-sense monoliths. I was with AT&T Wireless before they were bought by and subsequently merged with Cingular, and I wasn't pleased with AT&T's customer service or coverage. I decided to drop AT&T and get a free phone at Cingular with a two-year contract. I didn't speak with anyone at AT&T Wireless while canceling, I just asked Cingular to move my phone number to one of their accounts, which they were happy to do because I would be contracting with them to eventually give them about a thousand big ones (you should do the math for your contract too).

To make things complicated, the deal for the phone I wanted ended before my Cingular account was activated, and they couldn't complete the offer, which resulted in my throwing the phone across the room in a softball underhand manner. A month of haggling with customer service reps on a pay phone ensued, and I finally gave up on Cingular and went back to AT&T. Since it means more to these companies to acquire competitors' customers, I was offered an even better deal to go back to them with the same phone number that I had previously switched away. They gave me a free phone and a better rate plan for the same monthly price. I wonder, if I had continued to play this game of cell-company tennis, would I have eventually ended up with free monthly service or shares of stock?

The strangest aspect of this whole ordeal was that, during my negotiations, Cingular was in the process of buying AT&T and merging with them. I was bouncing back and forth between the two companies like the prey in a Night at the Roxbury dance scene and profiting from their competitive nature even though they were two divisions of the same company. It's like Coke paying you to buy Diet Coke instead of Coke Zero. Isn't corporate America fascinating? This is probably what Adam Smith had in mind when he said that companies would grow and improve in spite of the greatest of errors in administration.

The key to my success with the phone companies was their

desire for new customers (even though I was really an old customer for one of the companies). It just goes to show that corporate strategies for current customers and potential customers are vastly different. Companies can offer extraordinary deals to potential customers through advertisements and in-store deals because their current customers are in a contract and usually don't notice the great deals out there because they are happy with their service plans. If you are an existing customer and you want to speak to a live person at customer service, it may take half an hour, and you end up speaking to someone who can't pronounce your last name; but if you're a potential customer looking to spend new money, you're zipped right to the sales department and are chatting away with a David Hasselhoff impersonator within minutes.

If you have a problem with your service while you're under contract, you're treated like dirt; but when you decide to cancel your service after your contract is up, you get the most immediate attention-the retention specialists. These employees are empowered with every type of discount and deal that can be offered. Just like credit card companies, the cell phone retention specialists are the real dealmakers.

My most recent escapade into the world of cell phone bargaining occurred with a retention specialist. My contract had recently ended and I was receiving offers for free phones from my current service provider, Cingular. The problem was, that the free phones they were offering were made in the 1980s and resembled a shoe more than a phone. I was decidedly unpleased with the offers that they were giving me out of the kindness of their hearts, so I decided to shop around. I found that my airline miles credit card was offering cell phone plans with fairly nice phones that resulted in a free phone or in some cases, a free phone, and $50 cash back! In addition to the good phone deals, I would receive 4,000 airline miles. The deals weren't as good as I found on Amazon.com, however, and I was pleased to find a nice $425 phone there for free after a mail-in rebate. In this case, I would have to switch to T-Mobile, a company that has been said to have great customer service and Catherine Zeta Jones. My manhood may be challenged with all the pink on the phone, but I figured I could live with it since it was such a good deal.

Being the egalitarian that I am, I wanted to see if Cingular could match the deal. I called customer service, and the hapless representative couldn't give me a better offer to save his job. He kept repeating the same offers that weren't even as good as what I saw online. I asked him if he was a recording. He said that he wasn't and failed to see the humor. A week later, I called Cingular and found my way to the cancellation division. I asked them to match the offer and 20 minutes later, the very helpful young lady had a brand new $350 phone shipped to my house for free with a new rate plan that gave me more minutes than my previous plan had. This was after she couldn't complete the offer to charge me for the phone and credit my account the same amount. After all was said and done, she ended up crediting my account for the then-current balance in addition to the free phone. Needless to say, I was extremely happy for this helpful customer service and will recommend the company now wholeheartedly.

Sometimes, you can't wait for the pot to boil. If you're stuck in a contract and can't cancel to get to the great offers that non-customers get, there is an option for you too. You can get out of your contract without paying the hefty cancellation fees if, instead of canceling yourself, you encourage the cell phone company to terminate your contract, which they reserve the right to do. In order to encourage them to get out of this contract with you, you must make it unprofitable for them to be in the contract with you in the first place. If you have free roaming service in your plan (most contracts have that now), you can make it very costly for your provider.

Roaming occurs when you must use another network to make your call. When I was with AT&T Wireless, I was roaming all over the place, and Cingular or Verizon would pop up on my phone, indicating which provider's cell tower I was accessing. The roaming for my plan was free, but it wasn't free for AT&T Wireless. They still had to pay (up to $.69 a minute for some carriers). In essence, they were losing money on me when I was making a roaming call.

In most contracts cell phone service contracts, there is some fine print to explain that if you use roaming for more than 50% of your minutes, the company reserves the right to cancel your contract. So if you used 300 minutes non-roaming this month and 301 minutes roaming, they could theoretically cancel your account. With most carriers, roaming is rare, but if you can find a spot where your phone roams, you could turn the tables on your service provider. Of course, you should do this when your minutes are free (e.g. nighttime and weekends). This technique will take diligence in making the long phone calls while roaming, but it may be worth it to get out of the contract you're not in favor of.

Franklin Says:

"Having been poor is no shame, but being ashamed of it, is. "

The Culprit: marketers, retailers, brand name goods

The Target: natural urges of reciprocation, liking, respect for authority, social validation, and concession

Ad-In requires: self-confidence, math skills, patience

What Ben Earned/Saved:
- generic computer parts savings $190
- generic groceries savings (per mo.- nat. avg) $155
- 20% off Target.com bill $40
- rebate for printer $100
- free Pocket PC $350

Total $835

Part Six

The Information Age Wants to Help You

"The Internet will help achieve "friction free capitalism" by putting buyer and seller in direct contact and providing more information to both about each other."

-Bill Gates

"Like almost everyone who uses e-mail, I receive a ton of spam every day. Much of it offers to help me get out of debt or get rich quick."

-Bill Gates

20% off Timberland products. $200 off a trip to Hawai'i. A free camera flip-phone and free shipping from Cingular. What do all of these have in common? They are all coupon deals found on a website with hundreds of other deals that took the user two seconds to find. On another site for a popular airline there is an ad for Internet-only deals. Yet another website for a car dealership in Terre Haute, Indiana is also offering an Internet-only deal on a few of their cars. And they're all very good deals, which may lead to the question, why are there such good bargains online? Why do companies want so badly to draw us in online? The answer is that it's very profitable for them to do so.

For the same revenue dollar, retailers save money when they make an online sale as opposed to a sale at a walk-in store because they don't have to pay for customer service or the overhead for prime real estate. When accompanied by the fact that most prices for online purchases basically equate to their brick-and-mortar equivalents, companies are taking advantage of their consumers' increasing use of the World Wide Web.

While it's easy for a customer to make a purchase online, it's even *easier* for a retailer to make a sale. Once a store's initial site has been created (usually costing far less than a new building or annual rent), the update fees to place new items on the website are small and there is basically no maintenance to speak of, barring the occasional computer hacker attack. No floors to clean, no windows to wash, and no security guard to pay to stand watch. Most online companies don't even provide telephone customer service for their online marketplaces. They provide email service and perhaps a live chat feature, both of which are less expensive than a phone bank and, consequently, less efficient for the consumer. Online stores are cheap to start and cheap to maintain and that's why companies can and should offer you less expensive products or valuable coupons online.

Some would argue that along with the lowered cost of operating an online business, the retailers' options to direct customers to the site and advertise their products are also diminished. Christopher Preston of Queen Margaret University College in Scotland has argued that micro marketing, or marketing to specific consumers that have a high likelihood of buying your product, has major limitations. While traditional advertising like television commercials and billboards are aggressive and reach a large population, Internet marketing is more passive and selective in its target market. It has to wait for customers to happen upon an ad, while the old media advertising goes out and reaches out to customers.

I look at this dichotomy differently, however. Traditional advertising has to invade one's personal space to be effective. It has to break up a television show to be seen by the viewer or litter the subway to be noticed by millions of unsmiling commuters. On the other hand, Internet marketing is sought out intentionally. People actually look for advertisements on the web. That's why websites like AdTunes.com do so well in displaying companies' advertisements and critiquing them. It's why Google is becoming a media giant by selling ads that target its wide range of customers. It's also the reason behind some really bizarre behavior by Bud Light.

If you've listened to the radio much in the last few years or watched any sporting event on television, you've probably heard or seen one of the ads in Bud Light's *Real Men of Genius* campaigns. In the ads, a voice-over extols the virtues of people like the Mr. Basketball Court Sweat Wiper Upper, the Mr. Ceremonial First Pitch Thrower Outter, and who can forget the Mr. Fancy Coffee Shop Coffee Pourer? The Bud Light ads comically report the merits of these hilarious characters as in the case of the coffee pourer:

"What do you do with a Master's degree in Art History? You get a nose ring and pour coffee for a living."

"Why is it called a latte? Maybe because it costs a *latte* and takes a *latte* time to make."

"Sure you charge five bucks for a cup of coffee; it's putting that tip jar out that takes real guts."

This uproarious resume for these men of genius is accompanied by a mullet-sporting Richard Marx sound-alike and cheesy Eighties music, and it's a fantastically successful ad campaign by most measures. It's so successful that some people have made entire websites dedicated to the campaign. They have posted the ads in their entirety with disclaimers and all references to the company. Strangely, though, Bud Light has threatened many websites with legal action if they don't remove the advertisements. In a bizarre twist of marketing mystery, Bud Light worked to prevent one group of listeners from hearing the ads while they paid good money to have other people hear the same ads on other venues, like the radio. Most likely the Anheuser-Busch Company didn't want a third party getting web traffic and profiting from their property. But in essence, isn't that what radio stations do by charging companies to air their commercials?

It doesn't make sense for Bud Light to want to force a message on certain people (through radio and TV) and censor that same message from other people (on the Internet), a crowd that actually wants to hear the message. I find it baffling as it demonstrates that not everyone has quite grasped the power of marketing online or the full potential of the Internet in general.

Despite these exceptions, Internet marketing is growing rapidly as is web commerce. Based on the ease of buying and selling online, the move to an Internet-dominant economy is underway. The first quarter of 2006 showed an increase of 25.4% in eCommerce sales while the increase for all retail sales increased just 8.1%. First-quarter online sales surpassed $25 billion and, while the online percentage of overall retail sales was small, those sales are picking up steam, and that's good news for the consumer.

As mentioned in a previous section, the Internet can be a great asset to those who wish to take advantage of all the people and companies that are trying to take advantage of them. There are, of course, concerns about computers and the Internet. Some people say that computers are just keeping us from our friends and families, that there's only trash on the Internet, and that the Internet opens our kids up to a world of debauchery. Despite these criticisms, which may be valid to some extent, the information age is giving us opportunities that weren't even dreamed of ten years ago. There is unlimited value in the information explosion we call the Internet, and it's up to us to harness that value. So despite privacy concerns and other drawbacks with the Internet, I have been convinced that it is the greatest invention of all time because it increases knowledge and awareness exponentially, and that applies to all aspects of the invention including retail and eCommerce. Many would agree. In a study conducted at MIT, 87% of high school students and 89% of their parents said that the Internet was the greatest invention in the 20th century. No wonder Al Gore tried to take credit for it back in 2000.

Some people aren't as optimistic as I to anoint the Internet the greatest invention of all time. Though the potential benefits of the Internet are seemingly unlimited and we're nowhere near reaching them all, some people don't recognize that potential. Even Sir Tim Berners-Lee, who made major strides in the foundation of the Internet and the World Wide Web and has been credited with those inventions, has his misgivings. In an interview with the British Broadcasting Corporation in 2005, Berners-Lee was quoted as saying, "Even the clearest, cleverest and most comprehensive website can not hope to equal the wealth of information contained in a good reference book. The internet is most definitely not a substitute for a well-stocked public library." I couldn't believe this when I read it — maybe if it was spoken in 1995, but 10 years later? It's strange to think that the person given credit for something most people use every day doesn't fully appreciate it, but it seems that not everyone is on the bandwagon yet.

I find quotes like that to be akin to the major gaffs in spoken history. It reminds me of the statement by former President Rutherford B. Hayes in 1876, in which he said, "That's an amazing invention, but who would ever want to use one of them?" to Alexander Graham Bell after receiving a demonstration of the telephone. My personal favorite spoken blunder was by the Commissioner of the U.S. Patent Office, Charles Duell in 1899, when he said, "Everything that can be invented has been invented."

So, despite Berners-Lee's impression of the limitations of the Internet, I maintain that it's the best invention ever and can stand to benefit its users in a much greater capacity than any bricks-and-mortar structure. Understandably, then, the greatest invention of all time, which can help you find a hair dresser, communicate with your distant relatives, view your house from outer space, and enlighten you on pretty much any subject that has ever been discussed, should be able to help you with Ad-in. It just so happens, as you will discover below, that the Internet was practically designed to help you as a consumer take advantage of the people who are trying to take advantage of you.

From its inception, the World Wide Web was designated to be a free, updatable, and upgradeable information storehouse organized to encourage wide usage and increase the dissemination of information. The goal was to spread knowledge and provide the ultimate free-market democracy. That ideology has worked, and now 77% of all American adults use the Internet, usually to connect, save time, and get healthier. A recent survey of Web users showed that 85% of those on the Web use email to connect to others for work or social purposes. Maps and driving directions are popular as well, as is research on medical problems and medication.

Though saving money isn't on any of the major lists of Internet uses, it should be. The Internet is one of the easiest ways to save money and to benefit from Ad-in. From finding the absolute lowest price to making money on purchases by other people, the information age is there to help you out in your financial needs.

31. Chances are, you can find it cheaper

If you have gotten over the initial aversion to typing in your credit card number in a sometimes insecure network that millions of other people use daily and hackers are constantly trying to infiltrate, then you've probably made an online purchase or two recently. If this is the case, you are almost certainly aware of the vast marketplace that the Internet has become (eBay alone has 125 million users), and you should be convinced that if you have something to sell or buy, there is probably someone out there willing to buy or sell it. Amazon and eBay are the two most popular marketplaces online and can usually help you find whatever you want at a discount when compared to your local department stores.

The principle in play here is that increased supply and competition lead to more equitable and usually lower prices. When I recently received an email from Amazon.com for a good deal on a digital camera, I decided to investigate. I went to Froogle, which is Google's forum of online marketplaces, to see if it really was a good deal. Froogle is a way to find a particular product on the web and view all of the online stores that offer that product. Amazon.com was offering the camera for a nice price of $279.00, which I thought was a great deal. When I searched for the camera on Froogle, however, I was enlightened when I found a store in New Jersey selling the same camera for $100 less. However, another feature on Froogle showed that the New Jersey store's website had a seller rating of 2.5 out of 5 stars. It appeared that few customers had had a very good experience with that online retailer, so I moved down the list to see a number of like discounts, some with higher ratings. These were just the first few listings in a collection of 180 online stores that were selling the camera. I eventually came to the conclusion that the Amazon price was a pretty good deal after all.

Interestingly enough, the most expensive price for that particular camera was $899.00; over three times the Amazon price. It's my guess that that highly over-priced option isn't entertained much by Froogle's customers. However, if that price was all the customer saw and was the only available price for that camera, it's conceivable that that customer, and possibly many others, would think about buying it at the extraordinarily high price. Without anything to compare it to, it's easy for a store to overprice. The converse is also true: with a lot of competition, it's difficult for a store to overprice.

With the Internet, it's getting very difficult for companies to rip their customers off by gauging prices. Consumers now have the power to compare hundreds of options for a single purchase; they also have the luxury of weighing service quality and other extras along with price when making their choice.

32. Shipping discounts

For some items sold online, shipping can make a major impact on the end purchase price. Recent car trouble led me to an online purchase that demonstrated this. After the CHECK ENGINE light went on in my car, I got on the greatest invention ever (the Internet for those who haven't caught on yet) and looked up local shops that would take a look at my car. When I found that no one would look at the car without charging $90, I searched the Internet for other options. I found that I could figure out what was wrong with the engine myself by hooking up a tool called the OBD-II Error Code Reader. That way, I could get around the $90 diagnosis fee and just tell the mechanic what to fix. The OBD-II scanner cost about $30 in my local auto store, but I found it for $17.98 on eBay. Shipping for the part brought the total up to $27.98, but it was still cheaper than at the auto parts store down the street, so I made the purchase online.

Interestingly enough, I found out what was wrong with the car and called a number of mechanics and their coworkers to see if they could fix it. None even knew what the VFS A Pressure Output was, much less how to fix it. This process makes me wonder about the whole diagnosis process with auto shops, but I learned a number of things from this ordeal, not the least of which (and the one most appropriate for this chapter) is the seemingly hefty shipping costs for a lightweight OBD-II scanner.

That kind of price increase for shipping, 35% in this case, may deter online shopping and make the walk-in stores look more reasonable. Fortunately for online shoppers, there are online stores like Amazon, which has free shipping for sales of $25 or more. Some items are ineligible for the discount, but most apply and can end up saving you 20% of your final bill.

More than half of online retailers say that free shipping is their most successful marketing tool. That statement is reinforced by a 2004 survey that showed that 52% of online purchases were abandoned at the point when shipping costs were added to the total. Shoppers like the idea of getting their items online until they see what it would cost to deliver them. Amazon, no doubt, noticed this impediment to online shopping before it instituted the free shipping option. At first, though, they required a purchase of $99 or more to receive the shipping credit. They eventually brought it down to $49, and it appears now that they've found the most beneficial price requirement for encouraging sales: $25.

It's worked for me. I've not infrequently made an extra purchase to raise the total above the $25 limit for the shipping concession to apply. That extra item may have cost $10, but the shipping discount was probably $6 for both items, and I needed the extra item anyway, so it made sense to buy it as well.

The free shipping appeal is so strong, there are websites that provide that service alone. FreeShipping.com gives its members a rebate for the shipping of their online purchases up to $10 a purchase and $500 a year. This service is provided at $5.99 a month, which is approximately the same amount that many online retailers charge for a one-time shipping cost). While the unwieldy process of submitting your proof of purchase and an online confirmation of your purchase may be more extensive than you're willing to go through, it can save you money. The annual cost of $71.88 makes it cheaper than Amazon Prime, which offers free expedited shipping for all purchases at $79 a year.

On the other side of the equation, if you are an Internet seller or have an online store yourself, many websites and organizations offer free shipping materials to aid your efforts. The United States Postal Service and eBay have gone in together to offer free boxes to eBay sellers.

33. Start a website to receive discounts on online sales

This technique may not be for everyone, especially those who are not technologically inclined, however, it is a great way to get cash back on purchases you make at online retailers.

Internet markets like Amazon.com and BarnesAndNoble.com have affiliate programs in which third-party websites direct customers to these stores and encourage sales. These large retailers have elaborate programs that allow affiliates to create dynamic links that they may post on their sites to measure the traffic and sales that go through those links. The benefit to the third-party website manager who must post an oftentimes obnoxious-looking banner ad on his well-designed webpage is commission payment. When someone clicks from a third-party website, like Lots-of-ads.com for instance, Most items sold on a retailer's site as a result of a third-party click-through will fetch anywhere from 1-10% of the sale price and are given directly to the website manager.

The major retailers benefit from their programs with increased traffic, but if you have a website, you could benefit as well in that 1) you can make money or credits from other people who happen upon your site and click on to the online retailer, and 2) you can get rebates on purchases you make as long as you click through your own link. If you already have a website and a steady stream of traffic and don't mind altering the appearance of your site a bit, you could make some decent cash on that traffic. Otherwise, if you have the links up for your personal use or that of your friends and family, you can still get decent discounts on your purchases.

It is a fairly simple procedure to get started, though it's not clear how strict the online retailers are when it comes to whom they dish out affiliate memberships. They certainly look to gain traffic from your site, not just a couple clicks from you and your friends, but most online stores will be happy to get any increased traffic.

Another way to bank on your website is with ad revenue from the major online advertising companies like Google and Yahoo! If you have traffic on your site, it may behoove you to take the time to sign up for ad programs like Google's AdSense or the Yahoo! Publisher Network, which give businesses easy ways to advertise on their website networks. With modest traffic to your site, you could earn a few thousand dollars a year just on your visitors' clicks. It's important to note that Google and Yahoo! take fraud seriously and will terminate your membership if they determine that you are artificially inflating the number of clicks on your ads.

34. Why pay an extra $5 to fly?

Most online travel agents like Expedia.com and Travelocity.com offer flights from many carriers and can offer the best deal on the flight you're looking for. The service is great and part of why the Internet is so beneficial. What Froogle does for retail items, these travel agents are doing for airline tickets.

However, there is a slight discrepancy between Internet travel agents and Froogle—you actually have to pay for the travel agents. While it may not seem like you are paying for anything during your Expedia.com experience (they certainly don't make it obvious that there's a fee), you're paying an extra $5 to book through that site as opposed to buying the ticket directly from the airline.

After you get your search results from the travel agency, take note of the carrier that offers your flight of interest. Then, make an identical search on that carrier's website, and you should find the same flight for $5 cheaper.

It may be worth it for you to pay the extra $5 a flight so that you don't have to fill out your credit card and contact information on every airline website, but if you're like me and have an account on all those sites anyway, there's no reason to pay the extra money.

Some travel services have now gotten away from the booking process altogether and just offer a fare comparison. Yahoo!'s Fare Chase makes it easy to check the prices on a number of different sites including the ones listed above and others like Orbitz.com and Cheaptickets.com, as well as airline websites like American's AA.com and Fronteirairlines.com. The user types in the flight information including location and dates, then hits search. The website searches 5-10 websites and updates the lowest fare as it searches. It's entertaining to watch as the price drops throughout the search.

Fare Chase, along with the travel agents' websites, still offers a great service, but it may be beneficial to buy directly through the airline the next time you make a flight purchase.

35. The more email addresses the better

Many online retailers or service providers differentiate their customers by their email addresses, which is often the customers' usernames as well. Many companies will let you use one credit card or bank account for multiple accounts, but often restrict the use of one email to only one account.

A benefit that you can take advantage of while companies do this is to have as many accounts as you have email addresses. What's the benefit of this, you may ask? For one, you can take advantage of multiple free trial offers. Netflix is an online DVD rental company that provides a great service by sending you movie rentals on a subscription basis. For a monthly fee, they send you one to five DVDs at a time and you can keep them for as long as you'd like with no late fees. The best part about it is that you can start off your membership with a free trial. Netflix gives its customers a two-week trial, free of charge to test out the service, and, if you were so inclined, you could continuously receive two-week trials and cancel before you have to pay the monthly fee by using several email addresses. Keeping track of all the email accounts and passwords would be annoying and difficult to, but it can be done.

Another benefit to this is due to the fact that many companies, Netflix included, treat their potential customers and new customers better than their long-term customers. If you maintain an account for a number of months, you become less of a priority and the quality of service that you receive declines.

I was a customer for a while with Netflix when a popular movie, Star Wars Episode III came out and I was eager to see it. When I placed it in my list of movies to receive (Netflix calls it your Queue), it showed that there was a *long wait* for it to be sent to me. This means that there was a long list of people who had priority over me for that title.

My brother signed up for an account shortly thereafter, and when he placed that same film in his Queue, he noticed that it was immediately and miraculously *available now*. New customers get great service from companies because they want to make a good impression on you. That good first impression has a way of lasting in the mind of the customer even when the level of service diminishes over time, and so the customer continues to buy despite being taken advantage of.

This practice of bringing in new customers by making them a higher priority is great for sales and stockholders, but it's not very nice to the loyal patrons. A way to reduce the inequity is to start another account or have multiple accounts.

Netflix most likely frowns on this behavior, and they do their part to prevent it, but by treating their long-term customers worse than their potential customers, they are almost asking you to take advantage of their rules. You can't have two accounts under the same name and email address, but signing up for multiple emails gives you flexibility to have new accounts when you need to. New email accounts, it should be noted, are free and easy to obtain through portals like Yahoo! and Excite.

Another way you can capitalize on multiple email addresses is by taking advantage of free gifts that come with new memberships. As we mentioned in previous sections, companies want to bring in new clients—a lot more than they want to work to retain their customers. For this reason, new customers get perks that regulars don't. For instance, Audible.com, a great online audio book service, offers a free Apple iPod for every Premium membership account that users sign up for. The conditions are that the user must maintain his or her account for 6 billing cycles (which pays for the trendy MP3 player and then some).

I had already maintained a Premium account for some time when they introduced the offer for *new* customers. I promptly canceled my membership and signed up again, receiving the free gift as a bonus. It cost me nothing to start a new membership, and the main drawback is that I have to sign in to different accounts to access the different content that I've purchased. I just received my second iPod Shuffle after canceling and signing up again. I'm probably going to use another great online resource, eBay, to sell the brand new player and use the profit from that to pay for the next few months of my Audible membership. That's what I like to call successfully achieving Ad-in.

Franklin Says:
"Anger warms the Invention, but overheats the oven. "

The Culprit: Internet companies

The Target: unfamiliarity with technology, laziness

Ad-In requires: web skills, technology skills to create a website, multiple email accounts

What Ben Earned/Saved:
- free shipping $6
- website ad revenue (monthly) $100
- website affiliate royalties (monthly) $90
- savings on online flight purchase $5
- new account gift $65

Total $266

Part Seven
Death *of* Taxes

"The nation should have a tax system that looks like someone designed it on purpose."

-William Simons

"When there's a single thief, it's robbery. When there are a thousand thieves, it's taxation."

-Vanya Cohen

      Benjamin Franklin, one of our thoughtful founding fathers, who stressed the importance of frugality and industry, has been quoted as saying one of the most poignant and regrettably accurate maxims in all of history: "In this world, nothing can be said to be certain, except death and taxes." This may have been his attempt to lower tempers when Britain imposed taxes on their American colonies. Franklin wanted to reluctantly accept taxes like the Stamp Act, which imposed a charge on all paper and paper goods in the colonies, to encourage a stronger union between America and Britain. But upon realizing what kind of fervor there was in opposition to the excises, Franklin began to side more with the revolutionaries and against the taxes.

      After looking at the average American's tax liability today, it is amazing to think about the small amount of taxation it took the first Americans to revolt against. They didn't revolt over a 35% tax on one's income that we know today, but over a tax of just *three cents* per pound of tea. It was a tax without representation, which made it worse, but the comparison to modern taxes is still valid. The first Americans didn't want to pay $0.03 in tax, whether they had representation or not, and meanwhile we barely even scoff at thousands of dollars paid to the government each year.

The first Americans didn't want to pay any taxes on things they were already paying high prices for. Americans, at least when they think about it consciously, still don't want to pay taxes. As humorist Gerald Barzan has been quoted as saying, "Taxation *with* representation ain't so hot either." And citizens are revolting against the high taxes now, but unlike 1776, today's revolt on taxation is happening under the radar and works against taxes on *income*, not taxes on *tea*. Billions of dollars are being hidden from the Federal Government through tax shelters, in which legitimate banks and financial institutions try to trick the IRS and show losses for their clients, which would never occur if it weren't for the tax benefits that the IRS itself promotes. Evidently, it was true what Will Rogers had to say, "Income tax has made more liars out of the American people than golf."

Why would an unnamed wealthy person in this country lease 25-year-old public transit cars in Germany for millions of dollars just to have them leased back to the German city? He or she did this to show a loss in net income and reduce his or her tax burden. This type of thing happens all the time according to the PBS documentary, *Tax Me If You Can*, and, assuming that the total amount of money that the Federal Government charges is appropriate, a great amount of money that should be going to the government is not and the rest of us tax-payers are left to foot the bill. Charles Rossotti, IRS Commissioner from 1997-2002, said that $250 billion to $350 billion dollars that should be going to the IRS every year is being held back and that illegal tax shelters account for the largest chunk of that money. He said that the average American would have a 15% smaller tax burden if everyone paid what they should according to the tax code.

The problem is that the tax code is so extensive and cumbersome that not even the IRS knows what people owe. Neal Boortz, coauthor of *The Fair Tax*, explained that if someone were to call up the IRS call center for help on their tax return, they would get the wrong answer over half the time. That is to say that the IRS is wrong 50% of the time regarding the subject matter that we've entrusted and paid them to know. It's no wonder though — the U.S. tax code is 3.4 million words long. I'll repeat that astounding figure, the U.S. tax code is 3,400,000 words long. It is shockingly long. If you were to read one word of the tax code each second, you would need to read for two and a half years straight to get through it all. It's hard to imagine that anyone has ever read the entire thing and that leads me to believe that it needs to be changed.

There are a couple things that are important to know about the U.S. income tax system of which most people are unaware. The first is that the income tax was not what the Founding Fathers intended. If you were to ask your friends (and perhaps enemies) what the highest percentage for income tax in 1910 was, I'm sure you would hear a wide array of answers. You'd probably get a lot of 10% or 90% as people naturally would have expected it to be vastly different than today's 35% for individuals. Well, they would be right that it was different, but probably no one would tell you that the highest percentage tax on income in 1910 was 0%. They knew our government has existed since 1776 and governments need money, so they would naturally assume that personal income would be the source of those funds. They would be wrong.

The politicians of the early Twentieth century snuck in an

income tax amendment that made it legal for Congress to levy taxes on income for the first time since the Civil War. The only reason that it passed and was ratified in 1913 (which was a time of peace incidentally) was that the tax was meant for only the wealthy. Everyone making less than the equivalent of $382,198 only had to pay 1%, while the highest tax bracket was only 7% and that applied to people who earned the equivalent of $9,554,954 or more.

There was a problem, though. The Amendment to the Constitution was fairly brief and it gave a lot of power to Congress, which many people didn't expect. The entire Amendment reads as follows:

AMENDMENT XVI.

Income taxes authorized.

The Congress shall have power to lay and collect taxes on incomes, from whatever source derived, without apportionment among the several States, and without regard to any census or enumeration.

It should have included at the end, "without any concern for what the founding fathers intended for this great country," because it was directly at odds with what the United States was founded on (remember the folks who revolted over the 3¢ tea tariff?). But Congress soon caught on to their new powers that worked against our founders' ideals and eased into a more weighty tax structure. By 1918, everyone was paying at least 6% and the highest tax bracket was suddenly giving up 77% of their income to the Federal Government. What a jump!

When government can take money, they sure learn fast how to do it. The 1918 rate was likely influenced by the Great War, which threatened many of our Western allies. In times of war, just as it was with the Civil War, we citizens are more prone to pay our government more without making a fuss.

However, while wars have their way of increasing taxes, subsequent peacetime doesn't have the reverse affect. The tax brackets pretty much stayed the same after the war in 1920. After WWII, which saw the lowest income tax bracket at 23% and the highest at 94%, the rates stayed pretty much the same.

Another thing that people should be aware of with regard to taxes is that withholding from one's paycheck was not always the method of choice for the Federal Government in acquiring taxpayers' money. The withholding feature, which took effect in the early '40s, was only passed into law after Macy's CEO Beardsley Rummel helped engineer a plan to make it seem like everyone would be exempt from paying their taxes in 1942 if they were to accept the withholding strategy for 1943. This plan was just a smokescreen, however, and the Federal Government not only maintained their revenue over this transition it increased it 500%. Granted, this was wartime and the government needed to collect more to pay off the expenses of defending our way of life, but a 500% increase is remarkable considering people thought they were going to be exempt from paying income tax for a year. The boom was due in part to the new method of withholding taxes from paychecks.

The IRS, on their website, states that the tax withholding system, "greatly eased the collection of the tax for both the taxpayer and the Bureau of Internal Revenue." What it really did was reduce the awareness of the impact of income tax and encourage tax increases. Before the Rummel plan went into effect, taxpayers had to sit down in the beginning of the year and write out a check to the Federal Government for the entire tax burden they had for the previous year, directly from their savings. It was a dramatic thing to spend 20% of your annual salary in one quick moment and it doubtless weighed heavy on their minds.

These days, no one bats an eye at the amount of money they're giving up to the government because they just see a few numbers on their paycheck—they don't actually ever get to see the money that the government collects. In fact, many people think that the government *gives money to them* every year instead of the other way around. I hate to break it to any reader who believes this, but the small refund that you get after doing your taxes is not the government giving you money, it's you getting back a small portion of the amount that you've already given up to the government. The government never really gives anyone money unless they receive benefits without making money themselves. However, the contrived income tax withholding and refund system makes it seem like they're just giving out money.

This abstract way of collecting taxes through withholding makes the lawmakers' jobs easier and our wallets thinner. Meanwhile, the beast seems to get more abstract the more we know about it. Today there are six tax brackets with no one giving up less than 10% of their income to the Federal Government. There is an endless amount of deductions and credits and it takes people an average of 27 hours to complete their tax return. Neal Boortz equated the time spent on conforming to the tax code every year (5.8 billion hours for everyone in the US) as the entire lives of 8,700 people. The lives of almost 9,000 people eliminated just to pay our taxes every year. How dramatically tragic is that? How much more real goods could we produce given that time back? The thought is staggering.

How did the tax code get so large and convoluted? It seems to me that the enigmatic nature of the gargantuan tax code represents hundreds, even thousands of government employees' intentions to serve their constituents and the special interest groups that support them. The result is a vast ocean of tax brackets, credits, and deductions that affect different people at different times and encourages certain behaviors.

If you've spoken with your accountant about income tax

deductions, then you're probably familiar with the most common deductions like the mortgage interest deduction and the charitable contributions deduction. Money spent on a home or charity isn't taxable, so that amount is also deducted from your total salary, giving you less tax burden. These deductions are exactly what the aforementioned tax shelters are doing for sneaky businesspeople, but are legitimate in that they are actual expenditures and are promoted by the government. That's right, the government wants people to own their own homes and donate to charity and that's why they are in the code. Other popular deductions are medical expenses, property taxes, and job search costs. Someone can also deduct his or her union or professional dues, tax preparation fees, safe-deposit box rental fees, and moving expenses. As many laws go, it makes one wonder how some laws got on the books in the first place. For instance, the Federal Government allows you to deduct gambling losses on your tax return, almost giving the gambler an added benefit for behaving in foolishly risky ways.

On the other side of deductions are tax credits, which don't reduce the net income, but rather contribute to someone's tax payment. If a taxpayer's liability (what he owes in taxes for the year) was $10,000 and he gets a tax credit of $2,000, their final payment to the government would be $8,000. Credits are much more valuable than tax deductions because they represent concrete rebates, not reductions in your income bracket, and that's why the Child Tax Credit that will remain through 2010 at $1,000 means so much to Americans.

With deductions and credits, the government can influence behavior of us taxpayers, which, right or wrong, benefits certain groups and professions. The treadmill industry was happy when a clause went into the tax code giving a deduction to those people who purchased a treadmill that year (but only if the buyer was obese). LASIK eye surgery, which some people think of as a cosmetic operation, is now considered a medical cost and can be deducted. I'm sure that made those eye surgeons happy. Day camp is deductible, smoking-cessation programs are deductible, and your jewelry collection is tax deductible. All of these deductions make a certain sector of taxpayers happy and put additional tax burden on the rest of us. One man's tax *loophole* is another man's tax *liability*, evidently.

Probably the most influential US judge not to sit on the Supreme Court, Learned Hand, summed it up well in 1947 in one of his articles. While the tax code was shorter back then, it was still a monstrosity, compelling Hand to write:

> In my own case the words of such an act as
> the Income Tax . . . merely dance before my eyes in
> a meaningless procession: cross-reference to cross-
> reference, exception upon exception — couched
> in abstract terms that offer [me] no handle to seize
> hold of [and that] leave in my mind only a confused
> sense of some vitally important, but successfully
> concealed, purport, which it is my duty to extract,
> but which is within my power, if at all, only after
> the most inordinate expenditure of time. I know that
> these monsters are the result of fabulous industry and
> ingenuity, plugging up this hole and casting out that
> net, against all possible evasion; yet at times I cannot
> help recalling a saying of William James about certain
> passages of Hegel: that they were no doubt written
> with a passion of rationality; but that one cannot
> help wondering whether to the reader they have any
> significance save that the words are strung together
> with syntactical correctness.

To many readers, this is not enlightening—they already know

that there are some outlandish deductions that the Federal Government has no good reason to be involved in. To others, it may seem odd that the largest employer in the world chooses to benefit certain people and refuse to benefit others. Weight loss is deductible, but only certain weight loss programs. The diet plan I devised, the Evolution Diet, which has been effective and helpful to thousands of people is not on the list of tax-deductible weight loss programs. I'm not established enough to lobby for inclusion in that exclusive circle, so I can't benefit from its undeniable monetary benefits.

I think that is unequal treatment, but despite this entire explanation of why the current tax system is flawed and unjust, this book is not a meant convince readers of the mess that is the income tax. It's not meant to encourage the very real possibility of wiping the tax code clear and replacing it with a simpler form of funding the government and ensuring that everyone pays their fair share, though that is a valid interest. This book is about accepting the current obnoxious laws and taking advantage of them.

If you feel that it isn't right that someone should get a tax break to try to quit smoking when you don't get a tax break for not smoking in the first place, perhaps that sense of injustice will ease your concern about taking advantage of some of the other things for which the government is offering deductions. People are constantly taking advantage of the government and they are doing so because the government encourages it. Why shouldn't you?

The people who are taking advantage of the government aren't just the typical social welfare recipients; very wealthy people also take advantage of the government. Would you be surprised to learn that Ross Perot, former candidate for President and multi-billionaire businessman, paid less in taxes as a percentage of his income than the average American? According to Thomas J. Stanley and William D. Danko, cited earlier, the average American now spends 12.9% of their income on taxes. Ross Perot on the other hand, who makes more than 9,500 average Americans combined, gives up only 8.5% of his income to the government. The disparity is even wider when you consider what he pays in taxes as a percentage of his total wealth. The average American pays 11.6% of their entire wealth to the taxman each year, whereas Perot only pays 0.8% of his wealth.

The reason Perot can get away with paying such a small percent, according to Tom Walker of the Atlanta Journal-Constitution, is that he invests in tax-free municipals, tax-sheltered real estate, and stocks without realizing their gains. One reason that the average American's percentages are so high compared to the billionaire Perot's is because the average American doesn't save as much as they should. Another reason is that Ross Perot takes advantage of an institution that is trying to take advantage of him.

The last part of that statement may be heavily questioned or scrutinized by people who idealize government. It is my stance that government, in general, does what every other organization or corporation does: it tries to survive and grow. Unfortunately, this survival and growth costs everyone who is not warmly situated under the umbrella of government funding. Every time the government does something that you don't want it to do, it has taken advantage of you by taking your money as a citizen and used it for something that you don't agree with. And, as opposed to credit card companies and marketers who take advantage of you, government's job is a lot easier. Government officials don't have to use psychological tricks or gimmicks to get you to pay up, they just write a law and there's not much we can do but to comply. Of course, it is our duty to vote legislators in or out of office, but less than 1% of the current population voted for anyone who made income tax an amendment to the Constitution.

Until we get a say in what should be taxed and what shouldn't, it is our option to take advantage of the current system. Since the government and the politicians we've elected have written these techniques into law, one could argue that it's our patriotic duty to take advantage of the government and the tax code. Of course, it's not just the tax code we're suggesting you take advantage of, it's everything your government does that goes under the radar. There's a lot to cover, so, let's get started!

36. Take the time to itemize

Many people who have the ability to deduct from their taxable income at the end of the year to get a larger portion of their money back from the government don't bother. They may not know that what expenditures they can deduct for or they might not feel like spending the time compiling all the receipts and sorting them when it's tax time. It's understandable how someone could feel that way; Americans already average 27 hours in completing their tax return every year. At a reasonable $20 an hour, that makes the cost of doing one's taxes $540 in lost potential income and that doesn't even include the accounting efforts put forth throughout the year.

If you're not getting back more than $540 in your return (many don't), it's not really worth it to be so diligent in making sure the government gets only their share and no more. It makes you wonder if that mentality is what government officials were counting on when they made the process so difficult in the first place. Is it possible that tax-code policy makers envisioned a lazy public who would give the government more money in exchange for more free time? If you're at all cynical about government's motives, you may find that question to have an obvious answer. A summary of this process may reinforce the cynicism: 1) Government takes money you've earned before you can even say "rip off." 2) Government sometimes takes more than you owe.

3) Government puts in place a convoluted refund system that makes it difficult to get back any money that you overpaid throughout the year.

4) Government charges *you* interest if you underpay.

Regardless of government's motives, many don't even bother to get the money that they are owed. Amazingly, in fact, the home mortgage interest deduction goes unclaimed more than half the time for people who could claim it. With the home mortgage interest rate, we're talking about a potential tax savings of thousands of dollars, yet, a few hours in early April is more valuable to most homeowners. In this case, IRS officials really have done amazing things to take advantage of us taxpayers.

If everyone automatically received the deductions available through the tax code, the system would be more just. However, these deductions are being looked over by most of the people who need them most (you and me). It irks me to think that some wealthy people are intentionally avoiding their tax obligation, while other less well-off citizens are blindly donating more than their fair share to the government by not taking advantage of those deductions. However, I do understand that justice alone may not entice many readers and that money might make for a more compelling reason to act on these special tax code gems. You can make a major impact on your income if you itemize your deductions and resist the urge to take the effortless standard deduction. The reason you can do this is that there are seemingly endless deductions. The IRS categorizes deductions into these groups:

1. Medical and dental expenses,

2. State and local income taxes, or sales tax,

3. Real estate and personal property taxes,

4. Home mortgage and investment interest,

5. Charitable contributions,

6. Casualty and theft losses,

7. Job expenses, and

8. Miscellaneous deductions.

Those may seem pretty vague and general, though. A longer list of deductions can be found in the back of the book, but I'll go over some deductions that may help you lower your taxable income and some that may surprise you. You can deduct medical and dental expenses if they are over 7.5% of your gross adjusted income for the year as well as popular deductions like charity donations and state and local taxes (Federal taxes paid cannot be deducted, incidentally). If someone stole your antique clock, you can deduct that or if a mad antelope escaped from the zoo and rammed through your front door, subsequently getting trapped in your house and destroying everything you have (casualty losses must be sudden and unusual), you could deduct all of that. You can deduct work-related schooling costs and the gas mileage to get to that school. If you are a schoolteacher, you can deduct supplies that you purchased and if you're an Armed Forces Reservist, you can deduct travel expenses. Additionally, you can deduct union dues or dues to professional organizations that help you do your work.

Those are fairly obvious deductions, but some people have taken the often vague deduction system to the extreme, trying to deduct some bizarre things. Some people have suffered for it when their deduction was audited and rejected by the IRS, but others make sense and can find a place in the legal realm of tax reporting. While claiming your dog as a dependent is unlawful, a taxpayer in Dallas deducted his guard dog's food as a security expense. On that note, you can also deduct the depreciation of livestock or other animals, but incidentally, only if they're used for breeding.

A Spanish teacher, also in Texas, was able to write-off his television and cable expenses for the betterment of his occupation because of the Spanish-language channels. Deductions for improvements in occupational skills can even go beyond what most of us think as just. Chesty Morgan, a Detroit area stripper couldn't deduct her breast implants as a medical expense and was brought into a tax court, where a judge reprimanded her. He also did her a big favor and allowed her to deduct the expense of her enlarged bosom as a business expense. Interestingly enough, if Chesty had deducted her new flotation devices as a medical expense she could only write them off if they exceeded 7.5% of her adjusted gross income, whereas if they were a business expense, they only need to surpass 2% of her income—quite a difference.

The general idea here that Chesty and our Texan friends were trying to capitalize on was the deductions of the Federal Tax Code. They, like most of us make money and the government is allowed to take some of that income, thanks to the representatives around in 1913. However, when you purchase any of the diverse and bizarre collection of items that has been approved by the IRS as a deduction, your taxable income is reduced by that amount. The ultimate goal of this Ad-in technique is to reduce your taxable income by acknowledging these purchases on your income tax return and reduce your tax liability, preferably to zero.

37. Start a business

There are 15 million people who have businesses that are considered Sole Proprietorships, according to the IRS, and that number is growing. Those 15 million people are smart entrepreneurs who are quite possibly taking advantage of some major benefits to owning a business, particularly when they're the only person in the business. Whether you start a business to provide you with your entire income or you start a business to earn some extra money here and there, you can count on two major benefits to doing business as a sole proprietorship and also some drawbacks. If you are a financially stable person, you can stand to profit from this popular type of endeavor. If don't think you can start a business or you don't want any additional hassles, perhaps you should consider starting one based on a hobby or other interest you have. It's simple, educational, usually very fun, and can help you take advantage of an overly complex tax code.

The first major benefit is while you do business as a sole proprietor, you avoid a double tax on the revenue that you bring in. What is a double tax, you might ask. A corporation pays taxes on the money it makes and the money it pays to its employees. Those employees, then, pay taxes on their income as well—this is the second time an income tax would be applied to the same money (a double tax). When someone owns their own business, or have a sole proprietorship like a lemonade stand, the government views him and his business as one entity, making the double tax impossible. When he gets money for each cup of lemonade, he doesn't have to pay for the corporate tax, just his income tax.

You can look at it this way: when you spend a dollar at Wal-Mart, you are giving about 40-60% to the government, but if you spend a dollar at Joe Schmoe's Lemonade Stand, you are giving 10-35% to the government. The difference is widened even more when you consider additional corporate taxes that are levied on companies' profits. Joe Schmoe pays taxes just once on his revenue.

But, you might say, if I don't have a business in the first place, then I don't have to worry about the double tax, because I don't really notice it. This may be true because income tax is only taken out of your income dollars once, but the fact that your company is spending taxes on top of paying you your salary certainly affects what you make. When an employer hires someone with a $50,000 salary, they must consider the taxes (income, Social Security, Medicare) that they must pay additionally. This can add up and it restricts the amount they can offer their employees. If your company paid you as a contractor, you would get the full amount and the business would take it as a loss and not have to pay income tax or any other tax on it. They could pay you $65,000 for the same work you were doing at $50,000 and make money.

The other key benefit to opening a sole proprietorship is the ability for sole proprietors to count their business expenses against other income, say income from a traditional day job. That is to say that you can deduct the new lawn mower for your weekend landscaping company from the money you received from your IT job. This is where the stickiness comes into play with regard to all the tax deductions and write-offs. The IRS is very clear with how we can deduct certain expenditures from our income, but there are a wide variety of things you could be deducting if you only had the knowledge of what deductions were possible. Well, now you have that knowledge: http://www.irs. gov/businesses/small/article/0,,id=109807,00.html. The IRS website is surprisingly extremely helpful in sorting out what business expenses can be deducted and in which circumstances.

Looking over the website may convince you that it's not worth all the effort to sort out the appropriate deductions, but believe me, it is. If you have a business selling rare Italian gel pens with plastic propellers at the ends and you conduct a business dinner with a customer to explain why he should buy 50 million of them, you can deduct that dinner's expense from your pen-selling income or your income from your day job. In fact, you can deduct just about anything business-related as long as it meets two criteria: the expense has to be ordinary and necessary. In other words the expense has to be a common one in your industry and it has to be helpful to your business. Buying $3,000 shoes to impress your customers probably wouldn't pass as a legitimate business expense in the auto industry, but if you're reasonable, the government is more than happy to provide you with tax deductions galore in promoting your business.

Much of what you're already spending now *without* a business can actually be seen as a deduction in the eyes of the IRS. Thus, starting a business can automatically help you save money on your tax liability. And it doesn't take much to get started. In many cases, you'll have to file for a business license and if you're going to do business in a name other than your own, you have to file for a Fictitious Business Name with the local municipality, but those are generally small fees and reasonably hassle-free when you consider the amount of benefits you may gain from this Ad-in technique.

These are the kinds of things you can deduct when you own your own business:

- Filling up your tank to visit a client in Podunk
- Dinner at Claim Jumper for you and your best clients
- Sky box tickets at the stadium for your 10 business associates
- Tickets to a charity gala (if all the proceeds go to the charity)
- Your new computer that you do accounting on
- A portion of your home mortgage or rent (if you have a specific home office designated)
- Medical insurance premiums

The main trick is to start living your life with the intent to save money off of nearly everything you do. A sole proprietorship is a great start in making your taxable income next to nothing and it's actually promoted by the IRS.

If you're convinced that starting your own business would be a good idea, you may still be wondering what you could sell or do through your own business. Here are some ideas:

As mentioned before, you could contract with your current

company doing what you already do and save them money while being able to write off your commuting expenses, your home-office expenses, and the laptop you just bought to do your work on.

Another option is to start a business doing something that you find enjoyable such as a hobby. If you like gardening and know some people that could use your services, you can start a small business as a gardener. The IRS distinguishes businesses from hobbies by the expectation to make money. If you do not expect to make money, you can still receive deductions, but there is a limit to the amount you can deduct. Also, if you don't create a business out of your hobby, you can't still deduct losses from your hobby from your other regular day job income.

The IRS gives these factors to consider when deciding whether your hobby can be considered a business:

1. You carry on the activity in a business-like manner,
2. The time and effort you put into the activity indicate you intend to make it profitable,
3. You depend on income from the activity for your livelihood,
4. Your losses are due to circumstances beyond your control (or are normal in the start-up phase of your type of business),
5. You change your methods of operation in an attempt to improve profitability,
6. You, or your advisors, have the knowledge needed to carry on the activity as a successful business,
7. You were successful in making a profit in similar activities in the past,
8. The activity makes a profit in some years, and
9. You can expect to make a future profit from the appreciation of the assets used in the activity.

Other easy-to-start companies that should be considered are Internet-based companies, which we briefly mentioned before, and consulting—anything from wedding planning to dietary consulting. One self-employed business that I'm particularly familiar with is writing. The tax benefits from all of these are nearly as long as the 3.4 million-page tax code and they're simple to get started.

There are risks with starting a sole proprietorship business, however, and those risks vary from industry to industry. In a sole proprietorship, since you and your business are indistinguishable, your company's liability is yours as well. If you are driving around in your ice cream truck, which you use to run your company, Jen & Barry's Ice Cream, and you run over little Bobby's foot, his parents might sue. You might have been little Bobby's favorite ice cream maker before the accident, but after that and with your company's business structure, his parents could not only bankrupt your company and take away the truck, they could also take away your personal savings account and your house and your dinner. The liability doesn't end at the business side when it comes to sole proprietorships, just as the deductions don't end on the business side of your income. You and the business are one entity and that may cause some tension in certain industries. This is likely why most sole proprietorships are not in high-liability industries. Though, it's not impossible, it's unlikely that anyone will sue you and your website that makes money off of advertising click-throughs.

In the early nineties, real estate mogul and recent television star (reality television sex symbol?), Donald Trump had a series of unfortunate financial setbacks and his company went bankrupt as it couldn't keep up with the interest on hundreds of millions of dollars in loans. If Trump's business was a sole proprietorship, Trump would have been bankrupt himself, but he wasn't personally responsible for his company and he never had to declare bankruptcy for himself, enabling *The Donald* to go on to reclaim billion-dollar status. If you are in a risky industry and you don't want to jeopardize your life savings or your family's wellbeing, you should consider starting an S-Corporation or a Limited Liability Company. These business structures allow you to operate your company as your own without assuming the full risk.

38. Hire your spouse while you're at it

If your sole proprietorship gardening company or ice cream truck company is really taking off, you may consider hiring your spouse and reaping more benefits with regard to medical expenses. First, you must hire your spouse at a reasonable wage (which will be deductible) to do something worthwhile in the company, either to drive you to the jobs or to prepare your ice cream sandwiches. Then, set up a written benefits plan for your employees and employee's families. You'll have to pay payroll taxes on your spouse's income, but it could all be worth it to be able to deduct medical, dental, and disability insurance (as described in Internal Revenue Code Section 213(d).

39. The government wants you to pay yourself first

Since you were no doubt infuriated by the above description of the Federal income tax system and how unjust it is (that may be wishful thinking), you would certainly jump at an offer to avoid many of the drawbacks legally. With regard to investing, one of the major drawbacks is being taxed twice on your money, once when you earn the money, then again when you cash in on your investment gains. If someone were to offer you a way to invest some of the money you make without getting taxed twice, you would naturally jump at the opportunity, and some do. However, you may be surprised to learn that well under half of the eligible American workers take advantage of the tax-deferred retirement programs like traditional IRAs or company-sponsored 401(k) programs.

I was guilty of letting this opportunity pass me by up until recently and I still don't fully take advantage of the IRA, while I invest in other accounts, which will end up costing me a double tax. If you are in the same boat and haven't invested into a tax-deferred retirement account to its potential, perhaps the reasoning was similar: I don't need to save money for retirement because I'm going to win the lottery tomorrow. Or perhaps the reasoning was that other retirement plans (like the wad of cash under the mattress) are easier to control. Maybe you are looking for Social Security to provide for you, even though it's said to be financially wiped out by 2020. Or, again, like me, you have been deterred by the early withdrawal penalties that apply to traditional IRAs.

If those reasons were anything close to your reasoning as to why not to invest in an IRA or 401(k) plan, then you'll be just like me in feeling physically ill thinking of all the money you could have saved just by investing your money before taxes were taken away. In a hypothetical set up by Fidelity Investments, someone earning $50,000 a year would earn $810 more by investing $3,000 in a tax-deferred account as opposed to investing after taxes. That is to say, if persons A and B both made the same salary (putting them in the same tax bracket) and invested the same amount into their retirement plans, but person A invested before taxes and person B invest after taxes, person A would have more money to play with at the end of the year. They both would have the same amount in their retirement plans (having deposited equal amounts) and have to pay the same taxes on that retirement money when they withdrew, but person A wouldn't pay as much in taxes initially.

This alone should convince you that you should look into taking advantage of the government's kind offer to tax you just once on your money. If you invest in a tax-deferred account, you'll have more money to spend now or you'll have more money to invest, which, compounded daily over an entire career could reap substantial rewards. If your company has a 401(k) plan, chances are that your company will match some of your salary as a contribution to your account. Free money? Why didn't I think of that? After three years at my previous employer without jumping on this offer, I had to scratch my head and wonder what I was thinking.

My main concern was the 10% penalty for withdrawing early, but there are options that will help you get to your money without the hefty price. You can usually take out a loan from your account, which may sound silly since you'd theoretically be giving yourself a loan, but that's the way they're usually set up. If you pay off the loan (and interest), you avoid the early-withdrawal fees. The IRS will let you withdraw some of your savings without penalty to pay for medical expenses, tuition for you or spouse, or dependents, first-home purchase, or payments to prevent a foreclosure of your house.

Regardless of the emergency exclusions, I finally realized that I would take a 10% early-withdrawal hit if I needed the money, but my employer was going to be doubling my contributions, so the net gain would still be 80% on top of what I contributed and earned. In other words, I would be coming out far ahead of what I would be without depositing in a tax-deferred account, despite the early-withdrawal penalty.

If the penalties and restrictions are still a concern, there are other programs the government allows that help you avoid being taxed twice on your money. The increasingly popular Roth IRA allows you to contribute money after it's already been taxed and lets you take the money at retirement without being taxed then. The Roth IRA plan also lets you remove money without paying a second tax and without fees if certain guidelines are followed.

40. Do you really want to donate more money to the government?

Recently, in Riverside County, California, the government just got a sizeable donation from the good people who have done business with the county offices. The total donation was $585,728 and the money went to the state General Fund. One might think, that was nice of those people. Well, besides the fact that California's government budget is already bloated, the main problem with this donation is that the people donating to the cause of bigger government didn't really know they were donating it. The money was left in the county coffers by residents who never cashed their county checks or who never picked up their child support refund.

The balance on these unclaimed funds has been growing recently and some checks had been in the county's control for a number of years. The county said that they tried to notify these unwitting benefactors through newspaper ads and mailed notification. It was estimated that the notifications cost $35,000, which was taken from the total amount before it was handed over to the state.

What many people don't know is that there is a good chance that they or a family member has some unclaimed money held by the government and you don't have to wait for the government to post a small insignificant ad in the local newsletter. You can go right now to the Internet and see what kind of funds await you. The back of this book contains a list of Internet links to sites where you can search to see if you have any money coming to you. I wasn't able to find any unclaimed funds when I searched my name in California and Indiana, my two states of residence since childhood. However, I input my brother's name in Indiana's unclaimed funds resource and found that he is owed $141.43. That's not going to change his life, but it's not chump change either. I explained to him that I expected a nice little finder's fee.

I'm sure you've all received the spam emails telling you about the huge unclaimed purse that's waiting for you if you just click on their link. That email usually comes after three heartfelt emails from three different nice Nigerian people who need to deposit $29,000,000,000.00 into your bank account. You should ignore those emails—if there really is money out there, no one's going to put that much effort into getting it to you and they might just relinquish it from your ownership altogether as in the case of the Riverside County government showed.

41. Need a house?

When someone who has a mortgage that is insured by the Federal Housing Administration (FHA) and can't make their payments, their bank usually forecloses and the Federal Department of Housing and Urban Development (HUD) takes ownership of the property. Since the Federal Government doesn't have enough use for all the houses it takes, it must turn around and sell it at a fair-market price according to them, which tends to be a little less expensive than the real fair-market price. The benefit to the average Joe is that you can get a fairly nice deal on a house if it has gone through this process. Since HUD doesn't really want to hang on to any of its properties, the idea is to sell them even if it means going below the market price.

The HUD website has an easy-to-access database through all of their third-party affiliates, which contains all the residences currently available. I did a search in Cincinnati, Ohio after I couldn't find anything in a search of San Diego properties. What I found was 78 properties scattered all over the city and surely a vast array of quality. Homes built as recently as 1988 were on the Cincinnati list and quite a few were listed a major discounts compared to their appraised values.

For instance, the 1988-built property, which was a two bathroom and two bedroom house, was appraised at $80,000, but listed at $72,000. Many are listed at their appraised value, but some aren't and they all require a buyer, which means that, if interested, you could submit an offer well below what the appraised value is.

HUD isn't the only government agency that has gotten into the game. The Department of Veteran's Affairs, the Small Business Administration, and the Federal Deposit Insurance Corporation all have properties they want to sell to you as do six other agencies including the most obvious, the Internal Revenue Service.

And these federal agencies don't stop at houses; there are government agencies that want to sell you cars, boats, airplanes, stamps, art, jewelry, horses, park passes, computers, office supplies, furniture, and memorabilia along with houses and commercial property. Firstgov. gov has a list of links to items that you can buy from the government and some of it may seem surprising. When I was going through this website, I felt like I was on eBay. One of the pages is called souvenirs and has a photo of an adorable little stuffed animal on it.

Why our government is in the souvenir business will be left up to another author to explain, but the fact remains that, right now, it is a business and you should take advantage of it, in part because they're already taking advantage of you. Each government business is being subsidized by us taxpayers, which means you're already paying for a portion of all the items or services that the government offers, including housing, machinery, and fuzzy stuffed animals. For government eBay, type in http://www.firstgov.gov/shopping/shopping.shtml to your Internet browser window.

Franklin Says:

"Idleness and pride tax with a heavier hand than kings and parliaments. If we can get rid of the former, we may easily bear the latter."

The Culprit: government

The Target: confusion about the tax code, unfamiliarity with history, laziness

Ad-In requires: web skills, extra effort at tax time

What Ben Earned/Saved:
- reduction in tax liability by itemizing $3,500
- reduction in tax liability for business expense $1,500
- gain in tax-deferred retirement savings $810
- unclaimed funds from former residence $141.43
- HUD housing discount $8,000

Total $13,951.43

Part Eight

Think Outside the Box While You're Thinking Outside the Box

"You are getting this raise! I deserve this raise! Yes! Yeah! Why are you going to give me this raise? Why! BECAUSE I AM AWESOME! I AM AWESOME!"

-Dwight Shrute (from *The Office*)

"There's no way I can justify my salary level, but I'm learning to live with it."

-Drew Carey

In 2005, a temporary staffing firm called Accountemps compiled a list of the most worn-out workplace clichés. Among all the "synergies" and "core competencies" was one we all recognize—the obvious catchphrase, "Think outside the box." This corporate banality is an oxymoron in itself because the concept is supposed to promote originality and creativity, but does so in a repetitive and stale way. So many people are trying to think outside the box nowadays that it's become popular, according to many online blogs, to start thinking *inside* the box. The central idea of thinking outside the box is still valid, however, and can be used to creatively take advantage of the people who are trying to take advantage of you in the workplace.

When people think of taking advantage of their employer, they usually think of racking up their expenses on a business trip or using the company car to drive to Vegas for the weekend. Others may consider using the nice perks that some companies offer to their employees as taking advantage of their work situation or employer. This may be valid as there are certainly some companies that offer substantial perks. For example, Southwest Airlines offers unlimited standby flights to its employees; The University of Notre Dame offers free tuition to its staffers' children; and most Vail ski resorts provide free ski passes and lessons to their workers. While these perks may be valuable to employees in certain professions, they don't apply to everyone, and they don't require one to think outside the box in order to obtain them.

For those of you who are content with your workplace and don't feel that you're being taken advantage of, these Ad-in techniques are probably not for you. For the rest of us, who feel that we're underpaid; who realize that our superiors usually get credit for much of the work *we* do; whose bosses torment us with frivolous busy work and bureaucracy, making the workplace a maze of regulations and hoops to jump through in order to do our jobs, there are techniques we can use to maximize our time at the office and see more from our paychecks.

This section won't include ways to sneak home reams of paper or paperclips when your boss isn't looking. That type of behavior is unethical and not what I'm referring to when I write about Ad-in for the work place. The types of techniques that I do encourage range from psychological methods that will help you to gain monetarily at the office through an increase in salary or a more efficient use of your time. These techniques also work for supervisors whose subordinates are parasitic and take advantage of *their* work ethic. If you have people working under you who you feel may be taking advantage of you, these Ad-in techniques will help you to regain the advantage.

As a seasoned modern job-market veteran, I can tell you that workplace patterns, which result in your being taken advantage of, happen across the board in various types of work environments. I've been part of a billion dollar corporation where the president was a mythological figure located thousands of miles away; a small business where the job description never completely describes the job and where heavy lifting is commonplace for an accountant; and a sole proprietorship where I didn't know what I was selling until someone had bought it. In each case, as with most jobs in the working world, someone attempted to take advantage of my hard work and dedication to the company.

I'm certain that anyone with even just a few days of experience in a corporate environment can attest to corrupt individuals who feed off of less aggressive and less established employees. I'm reminded of a scene in the movie *Office Space*, a comedy that parodies the absurdities of the modern workplace. When closing time on Friday rolls around, the protagonist, Peter, decides to leave work early, turning off his answering machine in order to avoid his dreaded manager's request that he work on Saturday. In this scene we see Peter anxiously shutting down his computer while keeping an eye on the manager who is making his way around the office. Once Peter has frantically closed down all the windows on his computer, he peeks over the wall of his cubicle and finds that he's in the clear—no bureaucratic manager in sight. Peter turns to escape from the impending weekend workday and is confronted with, "Yeaaaaahhhh, hi Peeetteeer. Yeah, I'm gonna need you to go ahead and come in tomorrow . . . mmm'kay?" And to add insult to injury, Peter's manager informs him that he'll need to come in on Sunday too. "Yeahhhhh."

In this comical scenario, the antagonistic manager is portrayed as a do-nothing micromanager who is easily disliked. He is the typical manager who takes advantage of his position and benefits solely off of others' work. The resulting story shows Peter becoming a prominent figure in the company by taking an honest, though lazy, approach to his job and refusing to allow anyone to take advantage of him. It's nice to think that dealing with the waste and mismanagement in corporate life in a straightforward manner will allow you to advance in your company, and it's quite believable while it's funny. Peter goes on to conduct some disreputable activities, which negate his overall appeal as a protagonist, in order to become wealthy. But the moral of *Office Space* (if there is such a thing) is still valid: stand up for yourself in the office and you will be rewarded.

Part of not being taken advantage of is finding a way to get people to do what you want them to do. This may require some of the techniques written about in Part Five: The Marketing Game. While it may feel a little odd to use marketing and sales skills on your coworkers and boss, it may be the most efficient Ad-in approach. One way to encourage people in the workplace to do what you want is by using the principle of *consistency*. When you want someone to help you, try getting him first to simply say that he will help you. Just by stating that he will help you, you've set that idea in his head, and you pretty much have a guarantee that he will follow up. If you set a co-worker moving in the right direction in the workplace, even if just verbally, it will be easier to keep him moving toward your goal.

In a study conducted by Joseph Schwarzwald of Bar-Ilan University, it was shown that donations to a handicapped advocate organization were nearly doubled when volunteers asked the potential donors to sign a petition in support of the organization weeks before they asked for the donation. Once the donors got it in their heads that they were supporters of this organization via signing the petition, they felt more compelled to give monetary contributions later to back it up.

This principle applies to the workplace as well. For instance, if you want your co-workers to simply email you when they make a breakthrough on their *Theory of De-evolution* (or comparative project), achieving this will be infinitely easier if you extol the benefits of workplace interaction and have them all to sign a contract to increase communication between co-workers before you ask them to email you. When everyone is excited about co-worker communication, they'll even offer to email you when you want. If you convince people to agree to fulfill a small request that is obviously beneficial to them, you help shape their definition of themselves and make it easier for them to agree to a larger request along the same lines down the road.

Techniques like these can help you get what you need out of the people with whom you interact on a daily basis. In the cases that follow, you can use the examples presented to take advantage of those who are trying to take advantage of you. As mentioned earlier, most of the following techniques apply to an employee at any level, from a serf to the king in the corporate feudal system, to the owner or customers in a sole proprietorship transaction.

42. Ask for a raise

One of the most common mistakes employees make is to settle for the salary their employer wants to pay them. This is common because it's difficult to muster up enough gumption to storm in to the boss's office and demand an additional $10,000. Most people aren't looking to stir things up, and they're definitely not the type to demand things from other people. For most, a raise would be more than they think they deserve, and, while that is true for some, it's probably not the case for you.

The single most important advantage an employee has in his quest for some extra moolah is the fact that it would be difficult and costly to replace him. Even the bizarre, smelly mumbler who sits in the corner cubicle is worth a great deal to the company because to replace him would mean searching for candidates, interviewing, hiring, and training a new employee. That would cost quite a bit more than most raises you'd be in the running for, raises that you'd be elated with. So your salary remains the same, and your employer slowly begins to take advantage of you.

If you've proven yourself to your company and you usually exceed in annual reviews, you should have no problem achieving a pay raise above that which would cover inflation (generally around 3% a year). On the other hand, if you have not been the poster child for your company and have been a thorn in your supervisor's side for the last year, you may need to straighten up before asking the big cheese for some extra dough that will cover that nice trip to Hawai'i you've been dreaming of. You can easily assess which type of employee you are from the annual report your company gives you. If your company doesn't have annual progress reports for its employees, you should initiate the process by setting goals and working with your supervisor to track how you're doing.

On a scale of 1 to 5, where 1 represents a poor employee and 5 represents the brown-nosed go-getter that we all try to avoid at office functions, most people fall into the 3-4 range, which fits the ubiquitous bell curve. If you consider yourself a 4 or 5, you should feel very confident about asking for more money. If you're on the other end of the scale and interested in a raise, you may need to bring some soap and a sponge to work, because washing your boss's car might be your best bet.

Regardless of your status, there are things that you can do to help maximize your raise. First, figure out who is actually in charge of making the decision. Many people mistake their supervisor for the person in charge of monetary decisions. If you're like me, you've seen situations where a nervous, pocket-protector wearing co-worker has spent a lot of time and effort kissing up to his immediate supervisor, while another co-worker, the one with the really nice car and obnoxious laugh, just speaks with the vice president about his compensation. Your immediate supervisor may be a good proponent for you in the negotiation room, but nothing replaces a solid approval from the director or vice president. So, toot your own horn, especially to the higher-ups. Make it clear when you've done a brilliant thing like saved the company a million dollars or, more importantly, figured out how to clear the paper jam in the printer. Email the "team" a success story and carbon copy the V.P. Yodel very loudly every time you make a sale. It's an unfortunate truism in a crowded business world that the hardest worker isn't always the most lauded. You have to flaunt your value and, more specifically, you need to let the ones with the power know.

Second, you should encourage some of your co-workers (preferably those you don't like) to quit their jobs. This may seem like an odd and funny technique, but nothing stirs the monetary pot like a couple 'take-this-job-and-shove-it's' directed toward the supervisor. While it's not recommended to threaten to quit yourself to get a raise, you can capitalize off of your co-workers' departures when the boss starts to worry about his diminishing workforce. He'll try to keep the staff that he does have, which means keeping them happy, which means paying them more.

When I was working for the aforementioned billion-dollar international conglomerate, a co-worker decided to leave for greener pastures, and I suddenly got another opportunity at a different company. Soon after I packed up my things and moseyed on out the door, my brother, who was working for that same conglomerate, was given a nice 7.5% raise for all the nice things he had done for the company. While the supervisor wouldn't have admitted that my leaving had anything to do with my brother's raise, it was obvious to everyone that the company didn't want to lose two Morse brothers in one week. When co-workers leave, your personal stock immediately goes up.

Third, ask for a raise when the company needs you most. While you may get a nice raise just for your nice smile and pleasant fragrance, the increase in pay will be exponential if a project is approaching that only-you-know-how-to-complete-it phase. You probably don't want to intentionally set your company up for failure, but if the company has just recently gotten busier and you're going to be working more, it may be a good time to knock on the supervisor's door.

Fourth, you should have a backup plan. If you go into your boss's office and say that you need a raise to be able to feed yourself and your pet gerbils, you should have a backup plan in case he or she rejects your request. You may want to post your resume on a popular online job board or talk to friends about any job openings they may know about. If you are successful in finding a backup plan, which may entail going on interviews and receiving offers at competing companies, you'll be more confident in your negotiation and will really be able to mean it when you say that you feel underpaid. This is a good way to realize your true market value. If you know of another company that's willing to pay you just as much or more than you're making for doing something you're more interested in, you're ahead in the bargaining game. Again, it's not professional to threaten to leave, but you can hint at your other options without being immature and increase the chance of a raise

43. Ask for a higher salary in the first place

A lot of agonizing toil and worry over salary and promotions can be avoided if you get the salary you deserve right off the bat. A big mistake that people make during the interview process is accepting whatever salary the employer offers, when this amount is usually intended to be a starting point for negotiations. When a potential employer offers x amount, conventional wisdom says that you should ask for x + y. The worse the employer can do is reject your request, in which case you can accept the position anyway or ask if he likes insulting your pride.

Employers take advantage of a couple things when they offer a lower-than-market salary: 1) if you're unemployed, you're more willing to take whatever is offered, and 2) few people like to negotiate salary. This seems to apply more to women than men, however, because in a recent survey by Lisa A. Barron of the University of California, Irvine, it was shown that men and women act differently in the negotiation process. In the survey, 71% of male MBA graduates entering the job market said they deserved a *higher* salary than other prospects, while 70% of similar women said they deserved *equal* compensation to that of other prospects. In addition, 83% of the women respondents said that they would need to prove themselves on the job, while 64% of the men said that the interview was the proving grounds.

These figures show that, while most new hires should usually ask for more to start, women need to be more aggressive than they have been to match their male counterparts. In a separate Carnegie Mellon study, it was shown that men negotiate with their future employers eight times as often and, thus, end up with 7.4% higher starting salaries.

An interesting point to note, though, is the comparison between men and women when it comes to sole proprietorships. While men have, by far, more businesses considered to be sole proprietorships in the U.S., women tend to do better with the businesses they have. A study by the Small Business Administration showed that, from 1985 to 2000, women's sole proprietorships grew at an average rate of 4.1 percent compared to 2.2 percent for their male counterparts. This indicates that, while women may need to be more aggressive in their negotiations with employers, they seem to be doing a lot better than men in their self-employed ventures. Nevertheless, employers are looking to take advantage of the resistance of new female hires to negotiate, so it's up to the women out there to fight that trend.

44. Market yourself

As stated above, the best way to make sure you're appreciated at your workplace is by marketing yourself. While it may seem reasonable to believe that good work will merit a good appraisal, I've experienced the opposite far too often over the course of my short corporate experience. I don't know how many times I quietly did my job effectively and efficiently while a co-worker received praise for complaining constantly. It's quite possible that a co-worker of yours has caught your ire by doing the same thing. These co-workers are the ones that find problems instead of solutions. Instead of working around an issue or finding a way to fix it, they routinely complain to their supervisors, making themselves look diligent while not really getting anything done. Sure, the problem may be solved eventually, but it will take a lot more effort from everyone else to solve it while the complainer gets out of his or her duty, supposedly because someone else wasn't doing his or her job.

These characters seek out problems, not to fix them, but to blame them on other people so that the problem-seekers look better. They are in every office and every business situation and they are ones to avoid working with if possible.

It pains me to say it, but these three-toed sloths of the workplace actually have gotten one thing right: they know how to market themselves in the workplace. Sure, they're using malicious tactics, but they're getting the job done. I distinctly recall a co-worker of mine who fit this profile exactly. She didn't really like me, and I think this was because I was just so darned charming and wasn't stressed by the workload that we all shared. She was in charge of approving the material that I had worked on, and, when she evidently let some mistakes slip through, she subsequently complained to a supervisor that I was doing sub-par work. As a result, she received praise and a bonus, while I was reprimanded.

It took me a while to figure this all out, but eventually it became clear that I wasn't being vocal enough about all the great material I *was* producing. Meanwhile my co-worker had a direct hotline to the complaint desk in our manager's office. To market myself better, I should have used the marketing techniques explained in Part Four: reciprocation, consistency, social validation, liking, authority, and scarcity. Simple translations of these techniques into the workplace frame would include the following:

• Reciprocation: do something remarkable and ingenious at your job, preferably right before any type of performance review you many have.

• Consistency: get co-workers or supervisors to commit to a smaller version of what you ultimately want done. If you want a raise, tell your boss that you're aware that he wants his employees to be happy.

• Social Validation: though it may be painful, it is beneficial to include your superiors in social activities and gatherings. Make them feel accepted, and you may reap rewards. Also, let them know that it's *cool* to give big raises. Even bosses want to be cool.

• Liking: be the nice guy/gal around the office who everyone wants to be around and can talk to. But don't talk too much because the most important person in the workplace with regard to your paycheck may see excessive talking as unproductive.

• Authority: try to maintain a good relationship with your boss's boss. When you have a good idea, obtain the approval of your superiors before you promote it to everyone else.

• Scarcity: if you appear to be a hot commodity, you may receive more monetary compensation for the same work you would do than if you were seen as a dime a dozen. And go ahead and encourage the co-workers you don't like to quit.

45. Gain business for your company

If you're not ready to start your own business as discussed in the previous section, you could practice your self-employment skills by bringing in new business to your current employer. You may know of someone who needs the service or products that your company provides. If so, try to facilitate a business transaction between that person and your company. To make the most out of your networking genius, you should make clear the kind of prize you'll receive once you ensure a new multi-billion dollar contract for your company. Even if your friend or acquaintance is not a billion dollar client, you should feel comfortable asking for a percentage of the total eventual business deal.

You shouldn't feel pushy or aggressive asking for a cut of the money that your company is going to receive for the business. After all, some companies actually hire professional brokers to introduce the same kind of new business. These brokers usually require a written contract that states what percentage of the transaction they will earn with their referral. Average percentages of 0.5%-1% may seem low, but if the deal is large enough, the reward will be well worth it.

If there's potential for providing a number of clients for your company, you may want to consider a fee arrangement for referrals. While a percentage system may work well for single large deals, a flat finder's fee may be more appropriate if you bring in a small army of clients. Either way, a contract would certainly be beneficial to you if you were planning on bringing the bigwigs together for a tête-à-tête. If you don't establish your compensation before the meeting, you may end up with a nice pat on the back while the V.P. of sales and your friend, moneybags, buy each other dinner. Don't let them take advantage of you!

In addition, even if your company has only offered a shiny new pen for a substantial referral in the past, don't think that they won't make the pot sweeter if you have a really nice referral up your sleeve. If you have a good lead, ask for a written contract stipulating a monetary reward. Smiles and good annual reviews may feel good, but a couple thousand dollars in the bank may feel a lot better.

46. Raise your prices

If you are a small business owner and not an employee, the only way you can realistically get a raise is to charge your customers more. While this technique may seem difficult to accept, it is vital to a healthy business, and there is a good reason why every company raises its prices over time: inflation. It costs more to do business year after year. Though raising prices may feel contrary to good business practices, especially when your company is doing well, a small business owner is being taken advantage of if he follows the market and doesn't raise prices. If you have your own business and have maintained your prices for two years or more, your customers are taking advantage of the principle of Business Inertia, which says that successful companies tend to stay their course despite rising costs.

Most companies do this because higher prices mean irate customers or retailers. As a business owner, you may be compelled to explain that there's this little thing called inflation, and, until the United States Federal Reserve changes its entire economic philosophy in order to eliminate inflation, prices are going to continue to go up. Another approach may be to explain that demand is going up for your product or service, and that you can charge more because what you offer is better than anything else out there.

Even if you don't *need* to raise your prices, it may be beneficial to do so anyway. Friends and family have always told me that my web design business should have a higher value, though I couldn't contemplate raising my prices when I wasn't doing enough business even at the low prices. When I finally upped my prices and started charging a deposit before starting a new project, I realized a dramatic increase in sales.

If you get a chance to have an economist talk your ear off at a party, something that is surely a once in a lifetime experience, you may pick up on some interesting theories before you fall asleep in your neighbor's seven-layer dip. Price Elasticity is the ratio of the gain in demand over the loss in price. Most of the time this number is negative, reflecting a general increase in demand as the price goes down. Sometimes, however, the Price Elasticity of a product or service is positive, indicating that the value would decrease as the price decreases as well or, similarly, that the value would increase as the price goes up too. Goods with positive Price Elasticity are called Giffen goods or Veblen goods in economist circles. Their increased value is the result of a number of psychological factors.

Thorstein Veblen, the author of the Veblen effect, may have had an ostentatious neighbor who liked to show off his 1890s version of a Lamborghini or Rolex watch while the economist was devising his theory. If so, Veblen might have noticed that the perceived value of a $10,000 name-brand watch is much greater than an identical $1,000 generic version simply because something that's ten times more expensive *must* be worth the higher price. Along with that theory, Veblen also came up with commonly used terms such as *conspicuous consumption* and *status-seeking*, probably to describe his funny neighbor.

These types of products, of which Veblen's fictitious neighbor had many, increase in assumed value as their prices go up. This increase is limited to products or services that provide status. But that could include your product or service if you're crafty enough. I have been consistently amazed by the amount of money that people spend in the graphic design field just to have their company represented by a big-name advertising firm. Sure, the product those big-name firms offer is often high quality, but the only real difference between billion-dollar Omnicom and the sophisticated up-and-comer is price.

Sometimes even the expensive product doesn't match the quality of the cheaper product made by the lesser-known company. Paul Rand was a talented brand designer who came up with some very successful logos, such as the blue striped IBM logo and the UPS package logo. By the 1990s, his price tag was extremely high, but the design he came up with for the Enron logo was hideous. Sure, Enron had the satisfaction of having its logo designed by one of the industry's pioneers, but the logo stunk despite the dear price they paid to have it designed.

Even though it's not necessarily true, people feel that if they're paying 10 percent of what the big name is charging, they're going to get only 10% of the quality. By raising your prices to 80 or 90% of what the big name is charging, you'll earn a lot more credibility, regardless of the industry you're in.

Franklin Says:
"Hide not your talents, they for use were made. What's a sun-dial in the shade?"

The Culprit: workplace supervisors and co-workers

The Target: confusion about the tax code, unfamiliarity with history, laziness

Ad-In requires: web skills, extra effort at tax time

What Ben Earned/Saved:
- raise (annual) $3,000
- higher starting salary (annual) $1,480
- business referral reward $300
- raising small business prices (annual) $5,000

Total $9,780

Part Nine

The Final Four

"The only way not to think about money is to have a great deal of it."
-Edith Wharton

"If you can count your money, you don't have a billion dollars."
-J. Paul Getty

Until this point, we've gone over the major institutions that are trying to take advantage of you, and which, consequently, *you* should be able to take advantage of in return. However, there are several companies and entities that just don't fit into the category of a major institution yet, but they are trying to get your money. Here's how you can return the favor:

47. Let the time-share company treat you to a vacation

I can't speak to the merits of owning a time-share, though some acquaintances extol them constantly. I do recognize an opportunity to capitalize when I see it, though, and time-share companies offer just that.

A friend of mine was working at a telemarketing company, and she would receive a commission for every couple that she got to attend a local time-share presentation. When she asked me to attend, I complied with her request and agreed to take my friend to the presentation, which was to consist of a half hour video and then a one-on-one talk with a sales representative. Once the sales pitch was over, we would be able to choose between two complimentary gifts: a trip to either Cabo San Lucas or Hawai'i, including hotel and airfare. There was no obligation to purchase anything, and the company would give us the vacation package just for showing up and listening to their pitch. That was the plan, or so they said.

This seemed like a great deal on the surface, and it really was except for a few factors. While the initial presentation and video were fun, relaxing, and jovial, the one-on-one interview was very un-vacation-like. My friend and I endured about 20 minutes of the sleaziest, most intense sales pitch that has ever been conceived. While one worker was going around popping balloons to indicate each time a sale had been made on one of the time-shares, our interviewer told us that we shouldn't wait to buy a timeshare because we just didn't know how long we were going to live. I was flabbergasted, and I still have nightmares about the salesman's nasty demeanor and fake gold jewelry.

To top it all off, we weren't able to get the time off work needed to take advantage of the vacation that we had endured all mental torture to finally receive. The timeshare company didn't make it easy to take part in the vacation—it was only available for off-peak dates during the middle of the week. Unfortunately, we did not take advantage of these people who were trying to take advantage of us, but we could have. We could have enjoyed a week in Hawai'i if our work schedules were more flexible, and that would have been worth spending even a half hour with the monstrous salesmen.

48. Know your credit

For years, banks, credit institutions, and even landlords and employers have used a tool known as the FICO (Fair Isaac Company) score to determine if you are at risk of defaulting on any potential loan or transaction they may enter with you. Until recently, we consumers have been in relative darkness regarding the enigmatic score — unable to access it ourselves and not really knowing what these companies are actually looking at.

The Fair and Accurate Credit Transactions (FACT) Act changed all that when it was passed in 2003 as an amendment to the earlier Fair Credit Reporting Act. The FACT Act requires the three major credit-reporting agencies (Experian, TransUnion, and Equifax) to provide a free credit report to U.S. citizens every 12 months. This report shows what kind of state one's credit is in and can be extremely informative.

However, the FACT Act allows you to get a free credit report, but it doesn't require that those companies show you your credit *score*. The three credit reporting agencies will provide the score for a small fee ($10–$15), but some financial institutions are taking advantage of the understood value of the score and offering it as a free tool that you can check periodically in order to see how your score is being affected by your economic behavior. Washington Mutual credit cards offer an online service for their customers as an added bonus to attract them from other credit companies. This service allows customers to login at any time and receive the latest report on their credit activity. The service also shows the customers' FICO score for each month of the previous year, allowing users to track the ups and downs of their scores.

49. Become a Freq

I like to travel, and I enjoy flying when I do go on vacation. The amount of flying I do can be costly, but with frequent flyer programs there are ways to let your expenses work for you. The programs are usually free, and you might be able to receive benefits after your first flight. Some programs provide discounts on food, more legroom on your flights, or free flights to Italy for you and your family. If you are a doubter, you might be interested to know that a member of my family got exactly that last year, and I was treated to an amazing trip to Italy for free. She had accumulated all her miles, or reward points, by flying for work—flights that she didn't have to pay for and would have had to go on one way or another.

Most airlines expect that you will choose to fly only with their airline if you have a frequent flyer account, and it makes sense to do so—the more you fly, the more rewards you see. These airlines expect that, because of the reward potential, you'll check with them first if you have to book a flight, and that you'll fly with them even when you could have gotten a better deal with CheaperAir. If you have a frequent flyer account with every airline, however, you can buy the cheapest flight and still benefit. The rewards will take longer to accumulate when your flights are spread out among different programs, but don't let that deter you. The miles will add up eventually, and the benefit will be yours.

Other perks associated with frequent flyer programs are affiliate deals. Many frequent flyer programs, most credit cards, and major websites for that matter have affiliate programs, which will benefit you as much as them. These affiliates pay the airline to send them potential business and, in turn, the airline gives me miles and, eventually, flights or upgrades to first class. If that's not good enough for you, the affiliate partnership usually results in discounts with the affiliate companies.

I recently looked into the affiliates on my United Mileage Plus account and was amazed to see that they had affiliate programs with many of the companies I already did business with. I immediately took advantage of the rental car deals being offered through Hertz (30% off) and Marriott (a free night's stay) on a recent trip. All I had to do to capitalize on these offers was to click to each vendor's website and make a reservation with the United discount code. With those purchases from United's affiliates, I also picked up some miles, bringing me closer to my ultimate goal of flying around the world five times.

50. Enjoy what you have

For the last 49 techniques and hundred some-odd pages, I've described ways to profit off of a complex and often bizarre economic system. What's the point? The point isn't to make you a couple hundred dollars here or a couple hundred there. It's not my goal to make the marketers sweat more in coming up with stranger campaigns to get your business. And the point certainly isn't to encourage greed or selfishness. The point is to help facilitate happiness through the benefits that you receive from these techniques. After all, that's the ultimate goal for most people, right? These techniques are supposed to make and save you money and ultimately to bring you more happiness from that money. But, just like all the things that companies try to sell us, more money will only make us happier *if* we allow it to. We live and work in an ever-expanding economic machine that we can take advantage of *only* if we are happy with what we get out of it.

The next time you're in a shopping mall, take some time to look around and contemplate the vast collection of absolutely worthless stuff that litters the stores and kiosks. Sure, there is some stuff of value to you at the mall, but, for the most part, the contents of the mall are useless to you. From the cheap plastic jewelry at teenybopper stores to the variations of foot massagers at the gadget store, we are blessed (or plagued, depending on how you look at it) with seemingly endless choices as to how we can spend our hard-earned money. If you're a male who likes to shave his face with a manual razor, it used to be commonplace to have to put up with one blade that roughly chopped the facial hair from your cheek. In 1971, Gillette introduced the Trac II—the world's first dual blade razor. The next few decades played host to the almost comical *razor wars*, where Gillette competed with Schick, Norelco, Braun, and more to outdo one another and come up with a more comfortable shave. They're up to five blades on a manual shaver now and, evidently, you can shave in your sleep with no problems thanks to the serious technology on these new puppies.

The inevitable question is do we really need five blades? To some, the answer is yes, and, to others, the appropriate question is, why stop at five? Why not blow the roof off of the shaver industry with 10 blades? I'm sure that, eventually, the geniuses at Gillette or elsewhere will devise a way to get 100 little blades on one manual razor. I can hear the ad copy now: "The new Gillette Century takes each facial hair, braids it with its neighboring hairs, then cuts it into infinitesimally small units and converts the hair particles into lotion to smooth out the shave." Wouldn't that be something?

The Gillette Century will cost you just under the amount you paid for your new car, but it will give you one heck of a shave, and it will be great for the environment. Is it worth it? Gillette, and millions of other companies, will try their hardest to convince you that it is. They want to encourage you to spend your money on their extravagant items not because these items are clever or nice, but because they're vital to your existence, and you can't live with out them. Companies out there use your natural urges—social acceptance, impatience, the desire to seek out a bargain, liking, and more—to make money on you.

When you see the commercial for the five-blade razor with the fit man being shaved by a woman more beautiful than most people ever see in real life, you feel a funny little urge to go out and get the razor in order to be liked. In an unrelated instance, when you hear that 50% of Californian children aren't getting an education, whether true or not, you're compelled to support the politician who wants to double the amount of money being spent on such a successful system because you feel a sense of guilt. When you see that the new iPod is the hottest thing out there and everyone has it, that also stirs up a funny little feeling that compels you to buy it so that you'll be socially accepted. But the single most important human urge that companies try to harness when attempting to take advantage of us is our seemingly inescapable need for more stuff. It's natural to want to accumulate more things, and companies and other people in the business world are more than happy to help us fill our garages with the unnecessary disco ball and the surfboard that has only been used once.

Contrary to popular belief, I believe we have free will to do what we choose. This *in*determinism allows us to fight abstracted natural urges and to refuse to succumb to those urges. And while we shouldn't reject progress initiated by these urges, we should look at the system in a different way. When we, instead, act on the virtues of frugality, propriety, and industry (Ben Franklin would be very proud), we learn to be happy with what we have. This is the key to taking advantage of the materialistic monster. Let me show you how this is the ultimate Ad-in technique.

In the West, we have an entire population dedicated to making things better and faster and shinier. We're all involved too: Steve Jobs is trying to create the best computer; little Bobby down the street is trying to be the best Madden '07 player; Aunt Sue and Uncle Greg are trying to get the most out of their Social Security money; and I'm trying to write the most helpful book in the history of personal finance. All of this leads to a more refined and productive economy, but there is no concrete end to the process. IBM or Dell will eventually catch up to Apple (though probably just briefly); little Sally may beat Bobby when Madden '08 comes out; Social Security is running out for Sue and Greg, and they'll have to find an alternative source of income; and someone very soon will write a much better book than this. This endless cycle of finding a good solution, making it better, and leaving the previous situation in the history books is how our economy has been so successful. If everyone were happy with Windows 95 or the Ford Model T, we would still be using those antiques.

However, we're not content with those products, and thus, we've encouraged the market to produce Apple's OS X Leopard and Chrysler's hydrogen fuel cell car. Having written this sentence, it's likely that when you read it, even these state of the art products will be history as a newer version will inevitably replace it. This push for better things is good. It makes our lives easier and gives us more free time to look online for even more time-saving products. Also, the move toward the future is making us wealthier—while we still do as much or less paid work as we did a few decades ago, we're making more money, and we can buy dramatically more impressive thing-a-ma-bobs and do-hickies with that money. While a video cassette recorder (VCR) cost about $600 when the technology was new, one can buy a much more advanced DVD player/recorder for $140 today. A newer technology, the Sony Blu-ray disc player, is currently estimated at $999, but that too will eventually be reasonably priced. We're getting more for our work hour despite inflation, but one thing this progress isn't doing is making us happier. As Greg Easterbrook makes clear in his book, *The Progress*

Paradox, we are getting wealthier and living much better lives by all standards, but we're not happier than previous generations.

It could be that this industrial machine that is making life better doesn't want us to be happy about it. If we were happy about our situation, there would be a lot less motivation to move forward and pursue an even better existence. If we were happy with four blades on our shavers, why would we want to buy the five-blade shaver? The materialism machine doesn't want us to be *unhappy*, but it certainly doesn't want us to be content. Who would build better computer operating systems or cars if everyone were content? In this respect, the gigantic machine that is our economy is taking advantage of you and your discontent in order to keep going. Progress is the destination, and your discontent is the fuel that is carrying us there.

The catch is that you don't have to be discontented. You can be happy about what you have and still move the machine forward by demanding better products. When you can be grateful for what you have, you are turning the tables on the machine and taking advantage of the economy that expects you to never be happy for longer than it takes you to shave with a five-blade razor because here comes the six-blade. This Ad-in technique can't be quantified in dollar amounts, but perhaps that makes it the most valuable technique of them all. Just like the classic MasterCard commercials that list the price of items for a particular event, then list the result, which is inevitably "priceless," your happiness is priceless.

Franklin Says:

"Who is rich? He that is content.
Who is that? Nobody."

The Culprit: time share companies, airlines, and the economic machine

The Target: fear, loyalty, and discontent

Ad-In requires: steadfastness, patience, happiness

What Ben Earned/Saved:
- vacation by time share company $1,540
- free flight through frequent flyer program $274
- 30% discount on weekly car rental $84
- free night's stay from miles program $179

Total $2,077

Part Ten

Conclusion

"Economics is extremely useful as a form of employment
for economists."
-John Kenneth Galbraith

"Spare no expense to save money on this one."
-Samuel Goldwyn

We live in a bizarre economy that is built on feudal
corporations that fill their pricing and products with arbitrary discounts
and values designed to get the most out of every customer. Often these
perks and discounts are planned in offices thousands of miles away and
a thousand feet up from where the customer eventually participates
in the transaction. In the ground-level retail store, someone may take
advantage of a 30% off on lingerie deal at Macy's in Oklahoma City, a
discount thought of by a man in a high-rise office building in New York
who probably hasn't seen lingerie in 20 years.

This discount or deal is carried out by an employee who is
making approximately 1% of what the overpaid guy in New York is
making and whose only care is getting off work later to go hang out with
her friends at the mall. This bizarre situation, filled with bureaucracy

and abstraction, allows for us consumers to really capitalize on the multi-billion dollar corporations. It also requires us to be diligent in making sure we're paying only the value of what we're buying, nothing more. In this abstract system of economics, the mass-market sellers give us things in the hope of capitalizing on our human urges and enticing us to buy more of their products. It's easy to see, though, with such great figurative and literal distance between the place where the discount is thought up and where the transaction eventually takes place, that the consumer (you) can take advantage of the situation without the seller even noticing that you failed to fall for its marketing tricks. This distance is multiplied when more multi-billion dollar companies are added to the equation.

To demonstrate the abstract and arbitrary nature that typifies this advantage game in our current economic system, I'd like to share a recent transaction that I made with a rental car company. My United frequent flyer program (described in the last part) offered a discount for Hertz rental car, whereas I would receive a 20% discount and an upgrade on a weekly car rental. When I arrived to pick up my car, I explained that I had a reservation, though I didn't have my reservation number. The nice customer service representative typed like the Tasmanian Devil on his computer for about ten minutes, asked his co-worker a question, and then went back to slapping his keyboard. I figure he got in a couple emails to his friends and typed a short novel during this lengthy check-in process, but eventually he returned to helping me. He asked me what the discount was that I was expecting. Evidently, his computer showed a discount code for my reservation, but didn't explain what the actual discount was. The worker, seemingly competent, required me to fill in the blanks of as to my discount. Evidently, I could have told him anything, as he didn't know what the discount was for. I could have told him my discount code was for a stretch limo with driver for $5 a day (yeah right).

I did tell the representative the true discount I was expecting to receive, but somehow, I got an extra discount anyway. I'm sure this isn't what Bobby Hertz, Jr. had in mind when he made a deal with United to offer discounts to their frequent flyer members. It turns out, however, that Hertz tried to get the extra discount back (intentionally or otherwise) by overcharging on one of the insurance items I paid for. When I returned the car, I was charged an extra sum mysteriously and, had I not audited the receipt, I would have paid the extra fee. I got the small rebate from the customer service rep at the check-in, but this price alteration again demonstrates the arbitrary nature of pricing with major corporations.

It's not just Hertz Rental Car Company that has seemingly arbitrary pricing. The abstract nature of retail pricing is everywhere. Swedish economist Knut Wicksell said, "Retail prices are frequently regarded as exceptions both to the law of costs and generally to every rational process of price formation…" And it's not just retail stores that are plagued with nonsensical pricing. Our government has gotten in on the act too. For instance, California's government chooses to advertise avocados on billboards and on the radio through the California Avocado Commission, yet it hasn't spent a dime advertising independent authors like yours truly. Why the arbitrary selection of government subsidy? It's hard to say.

Still, this is the economic situation in which we find ourselves, for better or for worse, and with recent world events it appears that more and more people are looking to join us in our free-market system.

On Christmas day, 1991, one of the most influential countries in the history of the world ceased to exist. In Moscow on that day, the hammer-and-sickle flag of the Soviet Union was lowered for the last time and replaced with the Russian flag with bars of blue, white, and red. Not only was this a spectacular event for the Russian people, most of whom had lived with Communism for their entire lives, but it was also meaningful to the rest of the world. For the West, it meant a relaxation of sorts from the constant antagonism felt from the East during the Cold War. It meant another large trading partner would enter the sphere of the world economy. And it meant that 150 million people were joining the free world.

In the grand scheme of things, the fall of the Soviet Union meant that the experiment started by Marx, and fueled by Lenin and Stalin, had failed. Just three years prior to the fall of the Soviet Union, it looked as if the country was as strong as ever from the outside. The insiders knew the truth—with an economy that was struggling desperately, and a young generation that was apathetic at best toward the socialist state, the country was failing. Mikhail Gorbachev took the reigns as the General Secretary of the U.S.S.R. in 1985, after a decade of negative economic growth, and woke the country up to the realization that its system was declining. He instituted *perestroika* (economic restructuring) and *glasnost* (a level of political freedom). But even his efforts weren't enough to overcome the corruption and bureaucracy that had stifled the Soviet economy and a Cold War adversary that wasn't going to cower to another superpower; the country collapsed.

The result is a world economy that is more and more dedicated to personal freedom and individual choice. What the West understood, though we have our detractors, was that people work very hard to build something or serve someone if they can reap the rewards themselves and not ship them off to a nameless government. It may seem cold and heartless, but humans are a selfish species to a large extent, and we only do things if they will benefit us and our dependents.

Ironically, this selfish behavior has been proven to be the only way that everyone gets what they deserve. True, the capitalist economic system doesn't give everyone what they *want*—no economic system can do that—but a true market economy does serve everyone justly and give them what they deserve. Amazingly, despite the evident failure of socialism, socialist ideas continue to creep their way into the minds of free people as solutions to society's ailments. Yes we have more wealth than any civilization has ever had, but we achieved that wealth by working for it in a generally free-market system, not because we've hedged our bets with a minor welfare state.

Adam Smith, in *The Wealth of Nations*, wrote, "It is not from the benevolence of the butcher, the brewer, or the baker, that we expect our dinner, but from their regard to their own interest. We address ourselves, not to their humanity but to their self-love, and never talk to them of our necessities but of their advantages." Again, this may seem cold, but it's the only way that everyone can be treated justly. The baker makes the bread, not so that we may eat, but rather to have a product that others will pay him for. He may then use that money he receives to buy something that he wants.

This free-market system promotes work and, in turn, wealth. People must work and create things and do services in order to get the money needed to buy what they want. This process inevitably leads to consumer products like the five-blade shaver, the 60 Gigabyte iPod, or modern marvels like the Channel Tunnel between Britain and France. We, in the industrialized world, may marvel at the pampered and easy lives we live. Billions of people today live better than the richest king lived 300 years ago; plus we have expensive shows like *CSI Miami*, films like *Harry Potter and the Goblet of Fire*, and NFL football for entertainment, whereas the Enlightenment-era king only had lame court jesters.

Suffice it to say, we're wealthy, but we're also benevolent. The United States has the highest Gross Domestic Product of all nations and, fittingly, it is the most munificent, giving to the underprivileged countries of the world while maintaining a charity network within its borders that's larger than most countries' entire economies. Smith explains this in *The Theory of Moral Sentiments* by explaining that there is something in us that encourages us to give even when we don't stand to benefit. "How selfish soever man may be supposed, there are evidently some principles in his nature, which interest him in the fortune of others, and render their happiness necessary to him, though he derives nothing from it, except the pleasure of seeing it." But we can't donate to charities or underprivileged countries if we are poor; we can do this because we are wealthy enough to do so.

Our economy, however, isn't all peaches and cream. Just as the Soviet State wasn't a perfect representation of a Communist state, the U.S. and its free-world economic allies are far from the ideal libertarian paradises envisioned during the Enlightenment. There are massive amounts of corruption and impropriety within our system, and there are industries and institutions that are taking advantage of the very people that make the country and the economy work (you and me). While some of these institutions use moral methods to get what they want, some tend to be not so nice about it. When certain people have more power than they can handle morally, they become corrupt, and situations like the Enron debacle or the WorldCom disaster arise. It is important to acknowledge these situations and make examples of the people who are to blame and of those who helped bring down the criminals.

It is up to each and every one of us in the free world to stand up against injustice like that brought on by the Bernard Ebbers and Kenneth Lays of the world. Just as companies can only charge what we are willing to pay for something, they can only get away with the amount of fraud that we are willing to turn a blind eye to. So, we should stand up for justice, and we should applaud those who alert the world to fraud and corruption, like Sherron Watkins of Enron. Everyone needs to do their part to make sure that corrupt business does not succeed, but by no means should the exceptions to the rule in a capitalist economy dictate our entire perspective of the economic system. The system works, and, while people and companies may seek to take advantage of you and your very human economic traits, the system also allows those of us who put forth effort to actually take advantage of those who are trying to take advantage of us. Doing so is not a breeze, and it does require patience and organization, but, as you have seen in this book, it can be very beneficial.

Hopefully, I've succeeded in describing the financial institutions that have been taking advantage of you and the rest of us for decades, as well as the creative ways you can return the favor. Using the techniques of Ad-in, you should be able to capitalize on your credit cards, your bank, your car dealer, your housing situation, the retail universe, government, and the workplace, and end up with more financial returns and perks for the business you do with them.

However, it's important to use these techniques wisely and avoid biting off more than you can chew. If someone were to try all of the techniques in this book right away and ask for a raise at work just to quit his job in order to start his own small Internet business, then open up five credit cards, and try to buy a house and a car, it might be a bit too much to handle. If that enterprising person were to pace himself, he might stand to benefit more than he could have hoped for. Some of the techniques in this book can be applied instantly to your economic life (like defending yourself against psychological marketers), but others can take years to do the right way.

One of my favorite children's books is *Aesop's Fables*, and a particularly appropriate story of Aesop's is that of the overeager dog with a bone in his mouth. When he happens upon a reflective pool, the dog notices another bone in the mouth of his reflection and wants that one too. Of course, the dog loses his bone while trying to double his stock. During the time old Aesop wasn't writing clever little fables, he was rumored to be a genius economist who dabbled in the ancient Greek stock market (the NASΔAΩ), and his words should be heeded even today. Sure, it pays to be a little risky now and then, but to be foolish and greedy usually puts your bone at the bottom of a pool. I can tell you from experience that it's not fun to drop your bone. After being smart and patient with some of the investments I made on a 0% credit card loan, I became careless and made some bad decisions that hurt my pride as well as my wallet. The setback didn't prevent me from continuing to take advantage of those offers, but it did sting a little.

My brief carelessness shouldn't stop you from benefiting from all there is to benefit from in this economy. Most of the techniques in Ad-in don't require risk, and the ones that do are accompanied by appropriate caution. This book should be a great way to start capitalizing on the system, and having completed it, you're now on your way to a world of endless perks.

For years, the perks have been out there waiting to be taken advantage of, but the financial institutions have been in control. Now you can take control from those institutions and start to benefit from them. Unlike the former Soviet Union, where the government took advantage of its people forcefully, very little in our system is mandatory. Yet, we live in a capitalist society that allows people and companies to try to take advantage of us; and they will if you let them. It is not only possible to take some of that advantage back; it is vital as a member of this economy that you do so.

Using the Ad-in techniques, you can turn the tide in your personal financial interactions. The advantage is now yours.

Franklin Says:

"Gain may be temporary and uncertain; but ever while you live, expense is constant and certain: and it is easier to build two chimneys than to keep one in fuel."

It has been my pleasure to share with you the techniques of Ad-in and hopefully help create a healthier personal financial situation for you, the reader. Here's a summary of what sort of monetary benefits you would receive from these techniques (by Part). Congratualtions on your new-found wealth!

What Ben Earned/Saved:

• A penny a day with interest	$19,653.14
• The Debt Benefit	$4,815.95
• Making Money on Money	$554
• The Two Most Expensive Purchases	$48,150
• The Marketing Game	$835
• The Information Age Wants to Help You	$266
• Death of Taxes	$13,951.43
• Thinking Outside the Box	$9,780
• The Final Four	$2,077
Total	**$100,082.52**

Appendix

List of Federal Income Tax Deductions

1. Student loan interest
2. Half of the self-employment tax paid
3. Self-employed health insurance premiums
4. Penalty on early withdrawal of savings
5. Alimony paid, but not child support
6. Medical transportation expenses including tolls, parking, and mileage for trips to health facilities, doctor's offices, laboratories, etc.
7. Nursing home expenses that are primarily for medical care
8. Medical aids such as crutches, canes, and orthopedic shoes
9. Hearing aids, eye glasses, and contact lenses, LASIK surgery
10. Hospital fees for services such as nursing, physical therapy, lab tests, and x-rays
11. Equipment for disabled or handicapped individuals
12. Part of the life-care fee paid to a retirement home designated for medical care
13. The cost of alcohol and drug abuse and certain smoking-cessation treatments
14. Special school costs for mentally or physically handicapped individuals
15. Wages for nursing services
16. State income taxes owed from a prior year and paid in the tax year
17. Fourth quarter estimated state taxes paid by December 31
18. Personal property taxes on cars, boats, etc.
19. Taxes paid to a foreign government
20. Mandatory contributions to state disability funds
21. Points paid on mortgage or refinancing
22. General sales tax deduction (including tax paid on large items such as cars or boats) in lieu of the income tax deduction
23. Cash and non-cash contributions to a qualified charity
24. Mileage incurred in performing charitable activities
25. General casualty and theft losses in excess of $100 and totaling more than 10% of adjusted gross income
26. Education expenses you paid to maintain or improve job skills
27. A handicapped individual's work-related expenses
28. Professional journals, magazines, and newspapers that are job-related
29. Cost of safe deposit box used for investments or business
30. Seeing-eye dogs for the handicapped or guard dogs for a business
31. Required uniforms and work clothes not suitable for street wear
32. Union dues

33. Employment agency fees or commissions in certain cases
34. Home office expenses, if for your primary place of business
35. Job-seeking expenses within your present field of employment
36. Reservist and National Guard overnight travel expenses
37. Dues to professional organizations
38. Business gifts up to $25 per customer or client
39. Your moving expenses
40. Business expenses including travel, meals, lodging, and entertainment not reimbursed by your employer
41. Cleaning and laundering services while traveling for business
42. Tools for use at your job
43. Cellular phones required for business
44. Worthless stock or securities
45. Commission to brokers or agents for the sale of property or property management
46. Fees for tax preparation or advice
47. Legal fees to collect taxable alimony or Social Security
48. Hobby expenses to the extent of hobby income you included in gross income
49. Services of a housekeeper, maid, or cook needed to run your home for the benefit of a qualifying dependent while you work
50. Gambling losses to the extent of your gambling winnings
51. Accounting fees for IRS audits
52. Exercise equipment for an obese person
53. Amortization of premium on taxable bonds
54. Appraisal fees for charitable donations or casualty losses
55. Appreciation on property donated to a charity
56. Cleaning and laundering services when traveling
57. Contraceptives, if bought with a prescription
58. Costs associated with looking for a new job in your present occupation, including fees for resume preparation and employment of outplacement agencies
59. Depreciation of home computers
60. Employee contributions to a state disability fund
61. Employee's moving expenses
62. Federal estate on income with respect to a descendent
63. Fees paid for childbirth preparation classes if instruction relates to obstetrical care
64. Foster child care expenditures
65. Improvements to your home
66. Investment advisory fees
67. IRA trustee's administrative fees billed separately
68. Lead paint removal
69. Legal fees incurred in connection with obtaining or collecting alimony
70. Margin account interest expense

71. Mortgage prepayment penalties and late fees
72. Penalty on early withdrawal of savings
73. Personal liability insurance for wrongful acts as an employee
74. Points on a home mortgage and certain refinancings
75. Protective clothing required at work
76. Real estate taxes associated with the purchase or sale of property
77. State personal property taxes on cars and boats
78. Theft of embezzlement losses
79. Trade or business tools with life of 1 year or less

Unclaimed Funds Websites

Nationally- http://www.unclaimed.org/
Alabama- http://www.treasury.state.al.us/website/ucpd/ucpd_frameset.html
Alaska- http://www.revenue.state.ak.us/Treasury/UCP/ucpsrch.asp
Arizona- http://www.azdor.gov/ucp/Owners/search.asp
Arkansas- http://www.state.ar.us/auditor/unclprop/
California- http://scoweb.sco.ca.gov/UCP/
Colorado- http://www.treasurer.state.co.us/payback/second/index.html
Connecticut- http://www.state.ct.us/ott/ucplisting.htm
Delaware- http://www.state.de.us/revenue/information/Escheat.shtml
District Of Columbia- http://cfo.washingtondc.gov/cfo/cwp/view,a,1326,q,590719,.asp
Florida- http://www.fltreasurehunt.org/ControlServlet?ActionForm=GotoNewPublicSearch
Georgia- http://www.state.ga.us/dor/ptd/ucp/
Hawaii- http://pahoehoe.ehawaii.gov/lilo/app
Idaho- http://tax.idaho.gov/ucp_search_idaho.htm
Illinois- http://www.cashdash.net/owner.asp
Indiana- https://secure.in.gov/apps/ag/ucp/
Iowa- http://www.greatiowatreasurehunt.com/dsp_search.cfm
Kansas- http://www.kansascash.com/prodweb/up/disclaimer_page.php
Kentucky- http://www.kytreasury.com/up/u_prop.asp
Lousiana- http://www.treasury.state.la.us/ucpm/ucp/claim/simplesearch.asp
Maine- https://portalx.bisoex.state.me.us/pls/treasurer_unclaimed_property/tredev.unclaimed_property.search_form
Maryland- https://interactive.marylandtaxes.com/unclaim/default.asp
Massachusetts- http://abpweb.tre.state.ma.us/abp/frmNewSrch.aspx

Michigan- http://www.michigan.gov/treasury/0,1607,7-121-1748_1876_1912-7924--,00.html

Minnesota- http://www.state.mn.us/portal/mn/jsp/content.do?id=-536881373&agency=Commerce

Missouri- http://www.treasurer.mo.gov/search.asp

Mississippi- http://www.treasury.state.ms.us/Unclaimed/

Montana- http://www.missingmoney.com/

Nebraska- http://www.treasurer.state.ne.us/ie/uphome2.asp

Nevada- https://nevadatreasurer.gov/unclaimed/search/Default.aspx

New Hampshire- http://www.missingmoney.com/

New Jersey- http://www.state.nj.us/treasury/taxation/unclaimsrch.htm

New Mexico- https://ec3.state.nm.us/ucp/SearchUCP.htm

New York- http://wwe1.osc.state.ny.us/ouf/oufSearchForm.html

North Carolina- https://www.treasurer.state.nc.us/DstHome/AdminServices/UnclaimedProperty/Search.htm

North Dakota- http://www.land.state.nd.us/data/abp/abpsearch.asp

Ohio- http://www.unclaimedfundstreasurehunt.ohio.gov/

Oklahoma- http://www.ok.gov/unclaimed/

Oregon- http://mscfprod2.iservices.state.or.us/dsl/unclaimed_property/search.cfm

Pennsylvania- http://www.patreasury.org/search.htm

Rhode Island- http://www.treasury.ri.gov/moneylst.htm

South Carolina- http://webprod.cio.sc.gov/SCSTOWeb/mainFrame.do

South Dakota- http://www.sdtreasurer.com/default.asp?page=unclaimed_property_page&section=search_claim

Tennessee- http://www.treasury.state.tn.us/unclaim/index-find.htm

Texas- https://txcpa.cpa.state.tx.us/up/Search.jsp

Utah- https://www.up.state.ut.us/search.asp

Vermont- http://www.vermonttreasurer.gov/unclaimed/index.html

Virginia- https://www.trs.virginia.gov/propertysearchdotnet/Default.aspx

Washington- http://ucp.dor.wa.gov/

West Virginia- http://www.wvtreasury.com/sites/unclaimed/index.html

Wisconsin- http://www.ost.state.wi.us/home/UCPWeb/ucpsearch.aspx

Wyoming- http://treasurer.state.wy.us/search.asp

Approximate Makeup of FICO* Score

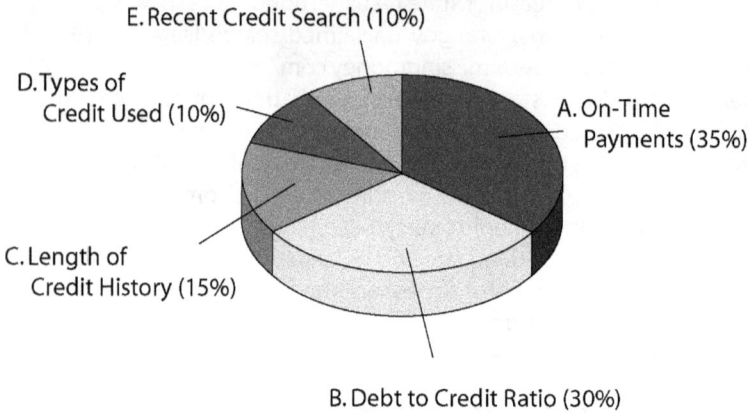

E. Recent Credit Search (10%)

D. Types of Credit Used (10%)

A. On-Time Payments (35%)

C. Length of Credit History (15%)

B. Debt to Credit Ratio (30%)

- 35% On-Time Payments: punctuality - payments later than 30 days past due
- 30% Debt to Credit Ratio: the ratio of current revolving debt (credit card balances, etc.) to total available revolving credit (credit limits)
- 15% Length of Credit History
- 10% Types of Credit Used (installment, revolving, consumer finance)
- 10% Recent Credit Dearch and/or amount of credit obtained recently

Notes

Introduction

A lot of debt: Ausubel, Lawrence M. "Credit Card Defaults, Credit Card Profits, and Bankruptcy." The American Bankruptcy Law Journal, 71 (1997): 249-270. Frugality: http://www.rideforlife.com/archives/000346.html, http://www.frugalfun.com/pphtoc. html, http://bygpub.com/finance/finance12.htm. Bad Pennies: http://www.msnbc. msn.com/id/5334880/. Interest Calculator: http://www.moneychimp.com/calculator/ compound_interest_calculator.htm. College-age Credit Card Consumers: Celia Ray Hayhoe, Lauren J. Leach, Pamela R. Turner, Marilyn J. Bruin, and Frances C. Lawrence. "Differences in Spending Habits and Credit Use of College Students." Journal of Consumer Affairs, 34 (2000): 113. Overcharged on Sale item: http://www.nevadaappeal.com/article/20060205/ BUSINESS/102050091. Debt: http://www.prweb.com/releases/2006/1/prweb331520.htm, http://www.theeastcarolinian.com/vnews/display.v/ART/2006/01/11/43c473730a64b, http://www.mastercard.com/us/securityandbasics/debtknowhow/payoffyourdebt.html, http://mymoney.gov/, http://www.ftc.gov/bcp/conline/pubs/credit/kneedeep.htm, http://finance.yahoo.com/columnist/article/millionaire/2406

The Debt Benefit

Economic games: http://en.wikipedia.org/wiki/Dollar_auction, http://en.wikipedia. org/wiki/Matching_pennies, http://en.wikipedia.org/wiki/Ultimatum_game. Cost of a dollar bill: http://www.cbo.gov/showdoc.cfm?index=5499&sequence=0. Credit cards ranked: http://www.indexcreditcards.com/, http://www.federalreserve.gov/pubs/shop/ default.htm. BBB on Bank of America: http://www.charlotte.bbb.org/commonreport. html?compid=100421; GM: http://search.detroit.bbb.org/nis/newsearch2.asp?ID=1&ComI D=0332000000004005;
Citi: http://www.newyork.bbb.org/reports/businessreports.aspx?pid=44&page=1&id=140. Chase: http://www.data.bbb.org/scripts/cgiip.exe/WService=wilmington/wilmington/ showrpt.html?zid=MAFpNjIfK. History of credit cards: Ausubel, Lawrence M. "The Failure of Competition in the Credit Card Market." American Economic Review, 81.1 (1991): 50-81. http://www.myfico.com/CreditEducation/WhatsInYourScore.aspx, "Secret History of the Credit Card" Narr. Lowell Bergman. Frontline. PBS. November 24, 2004. < http://www.pbs. org/wgbh/pages/frontline/shows/credit/view/ >, http://www.didyouknow.org/creditcards. htm,
http://newstandardnews.net/content/index.cfm/items/1524, http://www.finance.cch. com/text/c10s10d050.asp
http://smallbusiness.yahoo.com/resources/article.php?mcid=1&scid=10&aid=2018, http:// money.howstuffworks.com/credit-card.htm, http://smallbusiness.yahoo.com/resources/ article.php?mcid=3&scid=18&aid=2405, http://www.furia.com/vf/log.cgi?topic=43, http:// www.wilsonweb.com/articles/merch-cc.htm. Credit Report:
http://www.ftc.gov/bcp/conline/edcams/credit/ycr_free_reports.htm, Prakash, Snigdha. "Freddie Mac Exec Details Evolution of Credit Scoring." American Banker (March 6, 1997): 12A.

1. How low can they go?

Interest Rates: Calem, Paul S. and Loretta J. Mester. "Consumer Behavior and the Stickiness of Credit-Card Interest Rates." American Economic Review, 85.5 (1995): 1327-1336. Gross, David B. and Nicholas S. Souleles. "Do Liquidity Constraints and Interest Rates Matter for Consumer Behavior? Evidence from Credit Card Data*" The Quarterly Journal of Economics, 117.1 (2006): 149-185. Dagobert L. Brito, Peter R. Hartley. "Consumer Rationality and Credit Cards." Journal of Political Economy, 103.2 (1995): 400-433.

2. Ask for a lower APR

Lower APR: http://truthaboutcredit.org/truth.asp?id2=6153&id3=credittruth&. Credit card gimmicks and deals: http://moneycentral.msn.com/content/Banking/creditcardsmarts/ P79182.asp, http://www.pbs.org/wgbh/pages/frontline/shows/credit/more/battle.html.

9. Make money off of the credit card companies

High-yield Cds: http://www.bankrate.com/brm/rate/high_home.asp.

Things to Avoid

Dangers: http://moneycentral.msn.com/content/Banking/FinancialPrivacy/P87303.asp.

Making Money on Money

Banks: http://money.howstuffworks.com/bank.htm. Humphrey, David B. and Lawrence B. Pulley. "Banks' responses to deregulation: profits, technology, and efficiency." Journal of Money, Credit & Banking, 29 (1997). Inflation: http://inflationdata.com/inflation/Inflation_ Rate/AnnualInflation.asp, http://www.westegg.com/inflation/. Credit Calculators: http:// www.defenselink.mil/mapsite/ccardpay.html. How Banks make money: http://money.howstuffworks.com/bank4.htm. Banks' assets: http://www.netvalley.com/ netvalley/banks/top100assets.html, http://www.fdic.gov/bank/statistical/guide/. Bank fees: http://www.insiderreports.com/storypage.asp_Q_ChanID_E_CW_A_StoryID_E_ 20006529, http://moneycentral.msn.com/content/Banking/Betterbanking/P128196.asp.

10. Find banks that are willing to pay you to do business

Bank promos: http://www.bankofamerica.com/promos/jump/smbizreferral/referral.cfm, brits- http://www.credit-finance.iofm.net/bankoffer.htm, http://the.honoluluadvertiser. com/article/2006/Jan/12/bz/FP601120321.html, http://www.emoneycentral.com/. Virtual Banks: http://www.entrepreneur.com/article/0,4621,268144-4,00.html

11. Utilize online bill pay

http://www.indystar.com/apps/pbcs.dll/article?AID=/20060129/ BUSINESS/601290358/1003, http://www.line56.com/articles/default.asp?articleID=7261&T opicID=4. Protect against on-line fraud: http://www.fdic.gov/consumers/consumer/guard/index.html.

12. Try credit unions

http://www.mncun.org/CUAU.htm, http://www.bankrate.com/brm/static/compare.asp.

The Two Most Expensive Purchases of Your Life

Buying/leasing/new/used: http://www.edmunds.com/advice/buying/articles/47079/ article.html. Owning Versus Renting: http://www.signonsandiego.com/news/ business/20060125-1351-homeprices.html, http://www.ginniemae.gov/rent_vs_buy/rent_vs_buy_calc.asp?Section=YPTH.

15. Let someone else pay for your down payment

Stanley, Thomas J., and William D. Danko. The Millionaire Next Door: The Surprising Secrets of America's Wealthy. New York: Pocket Books, 1996.

17. Let the bank make money for you

Pricing: Poterba, James M., David N. Weil, Robert Shiller. "House Price Dynamics: The Role of Tax Policy and Demography." Brookings Papers on Economic Activity, 1991.2 (1991): 143-203. Home sales: http://www.boston.com/realestate/bigmove/articles/adsaying.html, http://www.nber.org/digest/mar05/w11053.html.

18. Try to buy without an agent

Using a broker: Zumpano, Leonard V., Harold W. Elder and Edward A. Baryla. "Buying a house and the decision to use a real estate broker." The Journal of Real Estate Finance and Economics, 13.2 (1996): 169-181.

Yinger, John. "A Search Model of Real Estate Broker Behavior." American Economic Review, 71.4 (1981): 591-605.

19. Decipher keywords on real estate listings

Real estate terminology: Levitt, Steven D. and Chad Syverson, "Market Distortions When Agents Are Better Informed: A Theoretical and Empirical Exploration of the Value of Information in Real-Estate Transactions." National Bureau of Economic Research working paper (2005).

20. Make the real estate agents work for you

Difference: Levitt, Steven D. and Chad Syverson, "Market Distortions When Agents Are Better Informed: A Theoretical and Empirical Exploration of the Value of Information in Real Estate Transactions." National Bureau of Economic Research working paper (2005): 7–8.

21. Let someone else help you build a real estate empire

Second Home: http://travel2.nytimes.com/2005/11/25/realestate/25rent.html?ex=1139634000&en=53671717e868c76a&ei=5070

The Marketing Game

Advertising Gimmicks: http://www.geocities.com/conspiracyprime/e2_leather.htm. CPI: http://www.thekirkreport.com/random_thoughts/, http://premium.econoday.com/reports/US/EN/New_York/cpi/year/2005/yearly/10/chart.gif, http://money.cnn.com/2006/01/18/news/economy/cpi.reut/. Sales: http://www.shopetc.com/shoppingcentral/besttips.vm. 350%: Cialdini, Robert B. "The Science of Persuasion" Scientific American, (February, 2001): 76-81. Coolness: "Hidden Motives" Narr. Alan Alda. Scientific American. PBS. March 2, 2005.< http://www.pbs.org/saf/1507/ >, "The Merchants of Cool" Narr. Douglas Roushkoff. Frontline. PBS. 2002. < http://www.pbs.org/wgbh/pages/frontline/shows/cool/view/ >. Marketing: http://www.greenchair.net/articles/viral-marketing.htm. Early adopter: http://www.firstadopter.com/. Similar cars: http://popularhotrodding.com/features/0510phr_nine/, http://www.businessweek.com/autos/content/jan2006/bw20060124_277216.htm. Grocery Savings: http://www.stretcher.com/stories/970303d.cfm.

22. Assess the value of your favorite brand

Coupons: http://www.couponcraze.com/. Consumerism: http://en.wikipedia.org/wiki/Consumerism. Generics: http://www.washingtonpost.com/wp-dyn/content/article/2006/02/03/AR2006020302598.html, http://retailindustry.about.com/library/uc/02/uc_stanley2.htm. Gas: http://www.eia.doe.gov/neic/brochure/gas04/gasoline.htm. Bulk: http://vegetarian.about.com/od/newfoodssubstitutions/tp/topbulk.htm, http://couponing.about.com/cs/grocerysavings/a/buyinginbulk.htm.

30. Need a new cell phone?

Cell Phones: http://www.amazon.com/exec/obidos/tg/feature/-/508597/102-8292506-5179336,
http://calpirg.org/CA.asp?id2=21486, http://money.cnn.com/2006/04/18/technology/business2_thirdscreen0418/, http://www.ag.state.mn.us/consumer/phone/CellPhone.htm, http://www.hearusnow.org/phones/consumertips/wirelessphoneservices/checklistbeforesigningupforcellphoneservice/, http://www.mysimon.com/Consumer-Reports-Cell-Phones/4002-9375-6311091.html, http://roaminghack.blogspot.com/, http://bigpicture.typepad.com/comments/2004/09/customer_acquis.html, http://www.consumeraffairs.com/news03/cell_phone_deals.html, http://news.com.com/Clash+over+cell+phone+fees/2100-1039_3-5623824.html,

The Information Age Wants to Help You

Deals: http://www.slickdeals.net/, http://digg.com/deals. Privacy: Cranor, Lorrie Faith, Joseph Reagle, Mark S. Ackerman. "Beyond Concern: Understanding Net Users' Attitudes About Online Privacy." AT&T Labs-Research Technical Report TR 99.4.3 (1999). Airline cheap first-class fare: http://biz.yahoo.com/weekend/firstcheap_1.html. Greatest invention: http://web.mit.edu/Invent/n-pressreleases/n-press-99index.html, http://www.cnn.com/2005/TECH/12/30/poll.results/index.html.
Tim Berners-Lee: http://en.wikipedia.org/wiki/Tim_Berners-Lee, http://www.inventionmysteries.com/article4.html. Usage: http://www.rrstar.com/apps/pbcs.dll/article?AID=/20060523/BUSINESS04/105230021,
http://biz.yahoo.com/prnews/060524/nyw134.html?.v=54,
http://www.edn.com/archives/1995/122195/26out12.htm. Internet: http://transcripts.cnn.com/TRANSCRIPTS/0312/27/cst.04.html, http://www.census.gov/mrts/www/data/html/06Q1.html, http://www.npr.org/programs/specials/poll/technology/. Poor customer service: http://www.npr.org/templates/story/story.php?storyId=4274891

32. Shipping discounts

Free Shipping: http://www.informit.com/articles/article.asp?p=467165&rl=1, http://www.nbc10.com/summercountdownarchive/9254024/detail.html

Death of Taxes

Taxes: http://www.hgtvpro.com/hpro/doing_business_sales_marketing/article/0,2621,HPRO_20165_3667826,00.html, http://www.pbs.org/wgbh/pages/frontline/shows/tax/view/, http://www.businesstaxrecovery.com/irs_charitable_deductions, http://waysandmeans.house.gov/legacy/fullcomm/107cong/2-5-02/Records/NSA.htm,
Carroll, Robert, Douglas Holtz-Eakin, Mark Rider, and Harvey S. Rosen. "Income Taxes and Entrepreneurs' Use of Labor." Journal of Labor Economics, 18.2 (2000): 324-351. http://www.articleteller.com/Category/Taxes/242, http://www.articleteller.com/Article/Tax-Deductions-for-Your-2005-Hybrid-Automobile/26677, http://www.verticalpulse.com/my_weblog/2006/01/the_american_re.html, http://www.fourmilab.ch/uscode/26usc/, http://www.ustreas.gov/education/fact-sheets/taxes/ustax.html,
History: http://www.taxfoundation.org/taxdata/show/151.html, http://www.ustreas.gov/education/fact-sheets/taxes/ustax.html, http://en.wikipedia.org/wiki/Income_tax_in_the_United_States. Adam Smith: http://www.adamsmith.org/smith/quotes.htm#jump1. IRS: http://www.irs.gov/newsroom/article/0,,id=110483,00.html. Contradictory rates: http://www.mises.org/fullstory.aspx?control=1597. Tax trivia: http://www.jacksonhewitt.com/resources_library_tax_trivia.asp. Credit report: http://www.ftc.gov/bcp/conline/pubs/credit/freereports.htm.

36. Take the time to itemize

Deductions: http://skbell1.statesmanblogs.com/tag.aspx?q=itemize, http://online.wsj.

com/public/article/SB114234406066997685.html?mod=tff_main_tff_top, http://www.
businessknowhow.com/money/50deduct.htm, http://www.irs.gov/taxtopics/tc501.
html, http://www.jacksonhewitt.com/resources_library_top50.asp?urlSection=resource,
http://www.bankrate.com/brm/itax/news/20020201a.asp?caret=34, http://money.cnn.
com/2003/01/29/pf/taxes/q_absurdmoves/index.htm. Charity: Adams, Burton and Mark
Schmitz (1984) The crowding out effect of governmental transfers on private charitable
contributions: cross-section evidence,National Tax Journal, 36, December, 563–7. http://
finance.yahoo.com/columnist/article/moneyhappy/4127

37. Start a business

Sole proprietorship: Mackie-Mason, Jeffrey K., Roger H. Gordon. "How Much Do Taxes
Discourage Incorporation?" Journal of Finance, 52.2 (1997): 477-505. http://www.
poznaklaw.com/articles/solep.htm,
http://www.inc.com/articles/2000/05/19685.html, http://en.wikipedia.org/wiki/Income_
tax_in_the_United_States. Business expenses: http://www.irs.gov/businesses/small/
article/0,,id=109807,00.html, http://www.smallbiztrends.com/2004/09/best-home-based-
businesses_09.html. Corporate taxes:
http://www.csmonitor.com/2005/0314/p17s02-cogn.html. Trump: http://en.wikipedia.
org/wiki/Donald_trump.

39. The government wants you to pay yourself first

IRA: http://www.irs.gov/retirement/article/0,,id=111357,00.html, http://www.freep.com/
apps/pbcs.dll/article?AID=/20060611/BUSINESS07/606110549/1020/BUSINESS, http://
partners.financenter.com/wamu/calculate/us-eng/rothira01a.fcs, http://www.timesleader.
com/mld/timesleader/living/14797815.htm,
Banks, James, Richard Blundell, and Sarah Tanner. "Is There a Retirement-Savings
Puzzle?" American Economic Review, 88.4 (1998): 769-788. http://www.dol.gov/ebsa/
newsroom/sp101503.html, https://401k.fidelity.com/401k/pfp/rp/fringe.htm, http://www.
edwardjones.com/cgi/getHTML.cgi?page=/USA/products/ira/individual_roth_ira.html.

40. Do you reall want to donate more money to the government?

Unclaimed funds: http://www.thedesertsun.com/apps/pbcs.dll/article?AID=/20060620/
UPDATE/60620010.

41. Need a house?

Government auctions: http://www.hud.gov/homes/homesforsale.cfm, http://www.firstgov.
gov/shopping/realestate/realestate.shtml, http://www.firstgov.gov/shopping/shopping.
shtml.

Think Outside the Box While You're Thinking Outside the Box

Worplace: http://www.mariosalexandrou.com/blog/index.asp?post=95.

42. Ask for a raise Rasise

Raise: http://www.hrwhatnot.com/articles/max-pay-raise.php, http://www.
personnelsystems.com/maxcomp.htm, http://www.cbsalary.com/MaximizeSalary. Deckop,
John R., Robert Mangel, and Carol C. Cirka. "Getting More than You Pay for: Organizational
Citizenship Behavior and Pay-for-Performance Plans." Academy of Management Journal,
42.4 (1999): 420-428.

43. Ask for a higher salary in the first place

Salary difference: http://www.hrmguide.com/rewards/women-negotiate-salaries.htm, http://www.womendontask.com/stats.html, http://www.csmonitor.com/2003/0317/ p15s01-wmwo.html. Lowery, Ying. "U.S. Sole Proprietorships: A Gender Comparison, 1985-2000." 2001. Oppenheim, Sara. "Gearing Up for Small-Business Push, PNC Building an Assembly Line." American Banker, (May, 1997): 1.

45. Gain business for your company

Finder's fee: http://www.businessweek.com/smallbiz/content/sep2005/sb20050926_ 032511.htm.

46. Raise your prices

Prices: http://www.entrepreneur.com/article/0,4621,308870,00.html, http://en.wikipedia. org/wiki/Price_elasticity_of_demand, http://en.wikipedia.org/wiki/Giffen_good. Leibenstein, H. "Bandwagon, Snob, and Veblen Effects in the Theory of Consumers' Demand." Quarterly Journal of Economics, 64.2 (1950): 1.

The Final Four

50. Enjoy what you have

Paid work: Robinson, John P., and Geoffrey Godbey. Time for Life: The Surprising Ways Americans Use Their Time. College Station, PA: Pennsylvania State University Press, 1999: 81-95.

Conclusion

http://oror.essortment.com/fallofthesovi_rkcm.htm
http://www.adamsmith.org/smith/quotes.htm
http://links.jstor.org/sici?sici=0022-1821%28198806%2936%3A4%3C375%3AATORP%3E2. 0.CO%3B2-A&size=LARGE

Bibliography

Ahearne, Michael, C.B. Bhattacharya, and Thomas Gruen. "Antecedents and Consequences of Customer–Company Identification: Expanding the Role of Relationship Marketing." Journal of Applied Psychology, 90/3 (2005): 574-585.

Altman, Edward I. and Anthony Saunders. "Credit Risk Measurement: Developments Over the Last 20 Years." *Journal of Banking and Finance,* 1997 (New York University Salomon Center Working Paper S-96-40).

Anderson, Chris. *The Long Tail: Why the Future of Business Is Selling Less of More.* New York: Hyperion, 2006

Anderson, Eric T., and Duncan I. Simester. "Are Sale Signs Less Effective When More Products Have Them?" *Marketing Scienc,e* 20.2 (2001): 121-142.

Arne, Larry P. *Liberty and Learning: The Evolution of American Education.* Hillsdale, MI: Hillsdale College Press, 2004.

Austin, Terry. "A Penny Saved May Not Be a Penny Earned." *Baptist General Convention of Texas,* (March, 2006): 1.

Ausubel, Lawrence M. "Adverse Selection in the Credit Card Market." College Park, MD, 1999.

Ausubel, Lawrence M. "The Failure of Competition in the Credit Card Market." *American Economic Review,* 81.1 (1991): 50-81

Bach, David. *Start Late, Finish Rich: A No-Fail Plan for Achieving Financial Freedom at Any Age.* New York: Broadway Books, 2005.

Barzun, Jacques. *From Dawn to Decadence: 500 Years of Western Cultural Life.* New York: HarperCollins, 2000.

Block, Sandra. "Childless, single renters can claim some tax deductions, too." *USA Today* 1 March, 2005.

Bortz, Neal, andJohn Linder. *The Fair Tax Book: Saying Goodbye to the Income Tax and the IRS.* New York: HarperCollins, 2005.

"Brain: Scientific American Mind, The." Digital Audio. Scientific American, 2004.

Brody, R., D Mutz, E Paul Sniderman. *Political Persuasion and Attitude Change.* Ann Arbor: University of Michigan Press, 1996.

Burton, Scot, Donald R. Lichtenstein, and Richard G. Netemeyer. "Exposure to Sales Flyers and Increased Purchased in Retail Supermarkets." *Journal of Advertising Research* (October, 1999): 7-14.

"CatoAudio, December 2005." Digital Audio. The Cato Institute, 2005.

Cialdini, Robert B. "The Science of Persuasion" *Scientific American,* (February, 2001): 76-81.

Diamond, Jared. *Guns, Germs, and Steel: The Fates of Human Societies.* New York: W. W. Norton & Company, 1999.

Easterbrook, Greg. The Progress Paradox: How Life Gets Better While People Feel Worse. New York: Random House, 2003.

Fair, Isaac. "Low to Moderate Income and High Minority Area Case Studies." Fair, Isaac and Company, Inc. Discussion Paper (October 4, 1996). *Federal Reserve Bulletin,* Table 4.23 Terms of Lending at Commercial Banks (February 1997): A68.

Feinberg, Joel and Jules Coleman. *Philosophy of Law, 6th ed.* Stamford, CT: Wadsworth/ Thompson Learning, 2000.

Fishman, Charles. *The Wal-Mart Effect: How the World's Most Powerful Company Really Works--and How It's Transforming the American Economy.* New York: Penguin Press, 2006.

Franklin, Benjamin. *The Autobiography of Benjamin Franklin.* New York: Dover Publications, 1996.

Freddie Mac Industry Letter (July 11, 1995).

Friedman, Thomas L. *The World Is Flat: A Brief History of the Twenty-first Century.* New York: Farrar, Straus and Giroux, 2005.

Gilbert, Daniel. *Stumbling on Happiness.* New York: Random House, Inc., 2006.

Gladwell, Malcolm. *The Tipping Point: How Little Things Can Make a Big Difference.* New York: Back Bay Books, 2000.

Gladwell, Malcolm. *Blink: The Power of Thinking Without Thinking.* New York: Little, Brown, and Company, 2005.

Glazer, Gwen. "Poll Track." *National Journal* 38.16 (2006): 68.

Group of 33, The. *The Big Moo : Stop Trying to Be Perfect and Start Being Remarkable.* New York: Penguin Books, 2005.

Hawkins, Jeff, with Sandra Blakeslee. *On Intelligence.* New York: Times Books, 2004.

Hayhoe, Celia Ray, Lauren J. Leach, Pamela R. Turner, Marilyn J. Bruin, and Frances C. Lawrence. "Differences in Spending Habits and Credit Use of College Students." *The Journal of Consumer Affairs*, 34.1 (2000): 113-133.

"Hidden Motives" Narr. Alan Alda. Scientific American. PBS. March 2, 2005. < http://www.pbs.org/saf/1507/ >

Internal Revenue Service. "2005 Instructions for Schedules A & B (Form 1040)." 2005.

Irwin, Robert. *How to Get Started in Real Estate Investing.* New York: McGraw Hill, 2002.

Isaacson, Walter. *Benjamin Franklin : An American Life.* New York: Simon and Schuster, 2003.

Johnson, Steven. *Mind Wide Open: Your Brain and the Neuroscience of Everyday Life.* New York: Simon & Schuster, 2004.

Johnson, Wendy, and Robert F. Krueger. "How Money Buys Happiness: Genetic and Environmental Processes Linking Finances and Life Satisfaction." Journal of Personality and Social Psychology, 90.4 (2006): 680-691.

Kiyosaki, Robert T., Sharon L. Lechter. Rich Dad's Before You Quit Your Job: 10 Real-Life Lessons Every Entrepreneur Should Know About Building a Multimillion-Dollar Business. New York: Warner Business Books, 2005.

Lawson, James C. "Knowing the Score." US Banker, (September 1995), 61-65.

Levitt, Steven J. and Stephen J. Dubner. Freakonomics: A Rogue Economist Explores the Hidden Side of Everything. New York: HarperCollins, 2005.

Lieberman, David J. Get Anyone To Do Anything And Never Feel Powerless Again : Psychological secrets to predict, control, and influence every situation. New York: St. Martin's Press, 2000.

Lowery, Ying. "U.S. Sole Proprietorships: A Gender Comparison, 1985-2000." 2001.

"Make Up Your Mind" Narr. Alan Alda. Scientific American. PBS. October 15, 2002. < http://www.pbs.org/saf/1302/index.html >.

"The Merchants of Cool" Narr. Douglas Roushkoff. Frontline. PBS. 2002. < http://www.pbs.org/wgbh/pages/frontline/shows/cool/view/ >.

Miller, John G. QBQ! The Question Behind the Question: Practicing Personal Accountability in Work and in Life. New York: Putnam Publishing Group, 2004.

Morse, E. Robert. Amazement: The Realization of Ideas and Dreams for a Sleeping Society. Lincoln, NE: iUniverse, 2002.

Morse, E. Robert. Justice And Equality. Lincoln, NE: iUniverse, 2003.

Oppenheim, Sara. "Gearing Up for Small-Business Push, PNC Building an Assembly Line." American Banker, (May, 1997): 1.

Preston, Christopher. "The Problem with Micro-Marketing." Journal of Advertising Research, (August, 2000): 55-58.

Robinson, John P., and Geoffrey Godbey. Time for Life: The Surprising Ways Americans Use Their Time. College Station, PA: Pennsylvania State University Press, 1999.

"Secret History of the Credit Card" Narr. Lowell Bergman. Frontline. PBS. November 24, 2004. < http://www.pbs.org/wgbh/pages/frontline/shows/credit/view/ >.

Shell, GR. Bargaining for Advantage: Negotiation Strategies for Reasonable People. New York: Penguin, 2000.

Smith, Adam. The Wealth of Nations. New York: Bantam Classics, 2003.

Stanley, Thomas J., and William D. Danko. The Millionaire Next Door: The Surprising Secrets of America's Wealthy. New York: Pocket Books, 1996.

Stanley, Thomas J. "Professional Wealth." Executive Summaries (2004): 1-9.

Stanley, Thomas J. and Murphy A Sewall. "Image Inputs to a Probabilistic Model: Predicting Retail Potential." Journal of Marketing, 40.3 (1976): 48-53.

Stewart, David W. "Speculations on the Future of Advertising Research." Journal of Advertising, 21.3 (1882): 1-18.

Stossel, John. Give Me A Break: How I Exposed Hucksters, Cheats, and Scam Artists and

Became the Scourge of the Liberal Media. New York: HarperCollins, 2004.

Stossel, John. *Myths, Lies, and Downright Stupidity: Get Out the Shovel, How Everything You Know is Wrong.* New York: Hyperion, 2006.

Sullum, Jacob. "Filing Fee." *Reason*, 38.1 (2006): 14.

Surowiecki, James. *The Wisdom of Crowds: Why the Many Are Smarter Than the Few and How Collective Wisdom Shapes Business, Economies, Societies and Nations*. New York: Doubleday, 2004.

"Tax Me If You Can" Narr. Hendrick Smith. Frontline. PBS. February 19, 2004. < http://www.pbs.org/wgbh/pages/frontline/shows/tax/view/>.

"Uncle John's Bathroom Reader." Digital Audio. Bathroom Readers Institute. Advantage Publishers Group, 2005.

Vaughan, Martin. "IRS To Stop Collecting Telephone Tax, Refund $13 Billion." *Congress Daily*, (May, 2006): 1.

Wantland, Robin. "Best Practices in Small Business Lending for Any Delivery System." *Journal of Lending and Credit Risk Management,* (December 1996): 16-25.

Williams, Janelle A. "Passing on the Wisdom of Wealth." *Black Enterprise*, (May, 2006): 65-66.

World Almanac Education Group, Inc. , The. *The World Almanac and Book of Facts 2006*. New York: World Almanac Books, 2006.

Zimbardo, Phillip G. , and Michael R. Leippe. *Psychology of Attitude Change and Social Influence*. Philadelphia: Temple University Press, 1991.

www.ingramcontent.com/pod-product-compliance
Lightning Source LLC
Chambersburg PA
CBHW071601210326
41597CB00019B/3341